IT'S NOT YOU IT'S YOUR PERSONALITY

SKILLS TO SURVIVE AND THRIVE
IN THE MODERN WORKPLACE

DIANE HAMILTON, PHD
& TONI ROTHPLETZ

ISBN: 0982742835
ISBN-13: 9780982742839

Library of Congress Control Number: 2010937160

DEDICATION

....

Our family has a lot of interesting characters in it. If not for them, we may not have had such a desire to understand personalities. For those of you who fall a little outside the norm (and you know who you are) ... thanks for the inspiration.

TABLE OF CONTENTS

INTRODUCTION –
PERSONALITY ASSESSMENTS

"I rely on my personality for birth control."

— Liz Winston

Why bother learning about personality? You can pretty much sum up whether or not a person is an idiot within the first few minutes of meeting them … right? Well, maybe. Just being able to recognize someone's personality disorder doesn't necessarily mean you're able to get along with them in your personal life or at work. One of our favorite George Carlin routines involves George assigning people into three personality groups. He claimed people were either Stupid, Full of It or Freakin' Nuts. We've cleaned it up a bit, but George did have a point! Ah we'll miss George. He really told it like it was.

So, if there are so many annoying personalities in the world, how are we all supposed to get along in society without wanting to kill each other? Part of what makes the world so interesting is that we're all diverse, and have our own unique qualities. However, because we're so ignorant of how personalities work, there can be conflicts. In this book, we're going to attempt to explain the importance of understanding personalities, why you should bother with personality assessments, and how to utilize this information in your personal life and at work to save your sanity.

This book is intended for the young adult or anyone looking to understand the different personalities of young adults. Why that group? Because over recent years there have been a lot of articles and books written about how the newer generations are changing. These generations are different from past generations in terms of what they want and expect out of life. If these newer generations are to get along with people, it's important for them to understand their own way of thinking, and how others think as well. This is a big part of being emotionally intelligent, which is something we'll also discuss later on in this book.

The term 'young adult' can be used to define those in their late teens to early twenties. For our purposes, we consider this group to encompass those as young as 16 all the way up to the mid-30s, and sometimes even older. For simplicity sake, we're going to call them NewGens. There have been many terms used to describe the generations since the Baby Boomers; Generation X, Generation Y, Millennial Generation, Generation Next, Net Generation, Echo Boomers, and so on. There also are mixed views on what dates should be assigned to Generation X, Generation Y, and the Millennials. According to CBS News, "There are about 80 million (Millennials) born between 1980 and 1995, and they are rapidly taking over from the Baby Boomers who are now pushing 60" (CBS.com, 2009). It simplifies things to lump all these groups together and call them NewGens.

Not all of the reporting regarding this generation has been flattering in terms of how their personalities differ from past generations. Many think that computers and technology have changed how newer generations think and what they expect, especially in the workplace. It has also been suggested that this generation has been pampered and rewarded whether they have deserved it or not. This has had an impact on their ability to interact in the workplace.

The goal of this book is to allow NewGens and anyone else interested in personalities and the assessment of personalities to look at all the different assessments out there and utilize the information from each of them to better understand themselves as well as others. Hopefully, the reader can come away with a sense of awareness that helps them be more tolerant of others around them. By understanding personalities, and what personality assessments can tell you about personalities, you will gain insight into why we all act the way we do.

Carl Jung, a pretty smart psychologist dude whom we will talk about in more detail later, is quoted as saying, "The meeting of two personalities is like the contact of two chemical substances: if there is any reaction, both are transformed." Through understanding how interactions affect outcomes, NewGens can gain perspective on how to utilize this knowledge to their advantage.

Before we can understand how personality assessments work, we must first define what a personality is. Sounds simple, right? Not really, however, if you really think about it. Ralph Waldo Emerson, who was a famous Boston poet in the early 1800s said, "There is an optical illusion about every person we ever meet. In truth, they are all creatures of a given temperament, which will appear in a given character, whose boundaries they will never pass: but we look at them, they seem alive, and we presume there is impulse in them. In the moment, it seems like an impulse, in the year, in the lifetime, it turns out to be a certain uniform tune, which the revolving barrel of music box must play" (Hughes, Ginnett and Curphy, 2009, p. 205).

If you're thinking to yourself, 'Huh?', you're not alone. Is the way we portray ourselves an illusion? Personality is not an easy thing to define, and can be ambiguous. Your personality may be seen as your social reputation, or the way in which others perceive you. However, there is the unseen part of what makes you distinctly different in terms of your behavior and how you react to things. Sigmund Freud, another famous old guy ... and if you've ever taken a college course, hey, even if you paid attention in high school, you should have heard of his name a time or two ... attempted to break down the personality into small sections such as id, ego, and superego. Freud saw these three things (id, ego, and superego) not as something physical in the brain, but rather as functions of the mind. The three are more or less self-explanatory, but we will quickly summarize.

The term 'id' isn't what you stole from your older brother or sister to get into bars before you were 21, but a component of personality that is present from birth. It is said to be the primary component of your personality, because it is your unconscious behaviors. It is the trait that meets your needs and desires. Think of it as like being hungry. What do you do when you're hungry? You go to the refrigerator and satisfy your hunger. Next, the ego satisfies the id's wants and needs in a realistic manner. It ensures that the impulses are met, but in a socially acceptable way. The superego is basically the judgmental component of our behaviors. Think of it as the morals inside you, determining right from wrong, good from bad. It acts to civilize our behavior. We're sure you can think of a few people who are lacking this component, but the point is, Freud believes that if there's a balance to all three of these elements, that's the key to a healthy personality. Often, those who are trying to define personality include a discussion of the key components and traits one possesses, such as in Freud's theory. "Although useful insights about personality have come from many different theories, most of the research addressing the relationship between personality and success has been based on the trait approach" (Hughes, Ginnett and Curphy, 2009, p. 205).

That brings forth the question, what are traits? Thefreedictionary.com defines a trait as "A distinguishing feature, as of a person's character." By understanding people's traits, we can get closer to understanding why a person acts the way they do. "Personality traits are useful concepts for explaining why people act fairly consistently from one situation to the next" (Hughes, Ginnett and Curphy, 2009, p. 206). Therefore, it is important that we look at the traits that make up one's personality to see how they play a role in one's behaviors.

Some people define personality as human nature, or differences in our individuality. Some suggest that these two things are the same thing. What exactly is human nature? It may be looked at as those qualities we have that make our particular species different from the rest. We all have motivations, such as the desire for status, for example, the desire to feel important, to be a 'somebody'. Some emotions that are part of human nature, such as jealousy, are universal; it's just that some of us can control it better than others. According to John, Robins & Pervin, "One way to define personality that captures most phenomena studied by personality psychologists is as those characteristics of individuals that describe and account for consistent patterns of feeling, cognition and behaving" (2008, p. 330).

One thing that many psychologists agree on is that we all have distinct personalities. Many famous psychologists like Freud have looked into what makes us unique in terms of our motivations. Psychologists have long looked into finding descriptive models or ways to classify people so that we can better understand personality. These descriptive models break our personality down into traits. How we reveal what our personality encompasses is through our preferences in terms of how we are motivated, and the way in which we cope with things. As humans, we look at the world in terms of outcomes and consequences. Because of this, we have to make decisions based on our motivations in order to achieve a desirable outcome. Our personalities include different ways of dealing with failure and success. Some people look at emotions as ways in which people view the world, that is, they can be thought of as our perspective on life.

What makes us all have unique temperaments and personalities? Today's researchers suggest it may have a lot to do with our chemical makeup, including things like serotonin and other big words that are hard to pronounce but have to do with brain chemicals. This brings up the debate about nature vs. nurture in terms of what affects our personalities. Are we born a certain way, or do society and our experiences change us somehow? Research has shown that your genetic codes do have an impact, but there is more research to be done to prove whether it is truly nature or nurture that defines us. There is also something called molecular psychology, which is about inheriting certain personality traits. Yep, that means our parents' lovely genetics could be the things that caused us to be so screwed up!

In trying to decipher personalities, there have been countless theories, and no end of theorists who have taken a stab at explaining personality. To be truly educated about personality theories, you really should know some of the top thought leaders in this area of research, as well as the highlights of their theories. We'll give you a quick rundown of some buzz theories and theorists that you should know about in order to have something cool to talk about at happy hour ... we're talking about the boring happy hours put on by work, that is. But don't worry, this will only be a brief history lesson, because if you're like either of us and weren't thrilled with your history class, we know you'll start to zone out quickly ... bear with us.

1. Probably the most discussed theorist would be Sigmund Freud, who was born in 1856 in the Czech Republic and died in 1939. If you've ever heard the word 'psychoanalysis' used, it's because of Freud, because that was his famous personality theory. He is famous for his model of the mind, which includes the three areas we discussed earlier: the id, the ego, and the superego. Just in case you weren't paying attention, your id is about how you derive pleasure, your ego is about how you make decisions, and lastly, your superego is about the moral aspects of your personality. You've probably heard the phrase "Freudian slip" at least once in your life. A Freudian slip is an error in speech, memory, or physical action that is interpreted as occurring due to the interference of some unconscious wish, conflict, or train of thought. As the common pun says, "A Freudian slip is when you mean one thing, but you say your mother."

2. Alfred Adler, who was born in 1870 in Vienna, studied social interest and how mankind can experience a feeling of "oneness". He felt people had choices that shaped their behavior. If you hear the term Adlerian

Theory, this is his work, which discussed how people strive for success. He felt creativity had a lot to do with one's style of life. If you've ever heard the expression "inferiority complex", it came from this guy. An inferiority complex involves having the feeling of trying to reach an unconscious goal in order to overcome feelings of inferiority and is thought to drive individuals to overcompensate, resulting either in great achievement or extreme discouragement.

3. You cannot discuss personality theories without looking at Carl Jung's work. Jung was born in 1875 in Switzerland, and felt that we inherited things that made up our emotional experiences. He called these inherited traits our collective unconscious. Notice a trend here? These theorists sure love to use that word 'unconscious' a lot! Some of his work on personalities was later developed by the mother and daughter team of Myers and Briggs, who made personality assessments popular in today's culture. We'll discuss this in more depth later. Carl Jung was once quoted as saying, "If one does not understand a person, one tends to regard him as a fool."

4. We need to get a female perspective here, so we can't forget Karen Horney (yes, that's her name, but it is pronounced 'horn-eye' ... seriously), who was born in 1885 in Germany. Ms. Horney created something called the Psychoanalytic Social Theory. This theory claimed that our childhood experiences shaped a lot of what our personality would be like in adulthood. She felt that one's environment had something to do with one's personality and disorders, and was quoted as saying, "The perfect normal person is rare in our civilization." Again, we can blame our parents if you

believe in this theory. Famous screenwriter and director Nora Ephron jokes, "[A successful parent is one] who raises a child who grows up and is able to pay for his or her own psychoanalysis."

5. Erich Fromm, born in 1900, also in Germany, created the theory of humanistic psychoanalysis. Part of his theory suggested that the fact that we don't have the same instincts as animals makes us stand out in the universe, sometimes in a negative way, with feelings of isolation or loneliness, etc. He felt the things that influenced us included our history and economics, as well as social and class structure. This guy had a quote that will keep you thinking for a while. He said, "If I am what I have and if I lose what I have, who then am I?" He is known for something called Critical Theory, which examined culture and society.

6. Interpersonal Theory was the work of Harry Stack Sullivan, born in 1892 in New York. Finally, some US representation! His theory claimed our personalities exist because of our interaction with others. In other words, f there were no one else around, we'd have no personality. I guess it's like the old saying, "If a tree falls in the forest and there is no one there to hear it, does it make a sound?" He felt the only way to truly understand personality was to look at how we interrelated with others, and was quoted as saying, "It is easier to act yourself into a new way of feeling than to feel yourself into a new way of acting." Sullivan developed the Self System, a configuration of the personality traits developed in childhood and reinforced by positive affirmation and the security operations developed in childhood to avoid anxiety and threats to self-esteem.

7. If you've ever heard of the term 'identity crisis', it's because of a guy named Erik Erikson. Why do people do that with their children's names? We never have understood the 'John Johnson' names. Isn't one John enough in a name? However, we digress. Erickson was born in 1902, in Germany. Those Germans were really at the forefront of personality study! Even though this guy didn't have a degree, he came up with what was called post-Freudian theory. Like many of the other theorists, his work was kind of an extension of Freud's, but he focused more on social and historical influences. He is known for saying, "Doubt is the brother of shame." He believed that any struggle or crisis that occurs contributes to our personality formation.

8. Starting with a guy named Abraham Maslow, theories later became more humanistic and existential or having to do with existence. Maslow was born in 1908 in Brooklyn ... another New Yorker steps up! If you've ever taken a business course, you will have heard of Maslow's Hierarchy of Needs. Maslow was all about understanding those things that create self-actualization, and proposed that we think of human needs as a pyramid. On the bottom you have basic needs such as physiological (the need for air, food, water, etc.), then the next level up on the pyramid is safety, followed by love/being, then esteem, and lastly self-actualization. Maslow is famous for saying many things, but the following is one that we like to quote: "If you plan on being anything less than you are capable of being, you will probably be unhappy all the days of your life."

9. After Maslow, a guy named Carl Rogers developed a theory called Client-Centered Theory. Rogers was

born in 1902 in Illinois, and was more of a therapist than a theorist, but he built his theory upon what he learned as a therapist. He felt that people strive toward goals that set them apart. He once said, "The curious paradox is that when I accept myself just as I am, then I can change." He later had a very famous debate with another important theorist named B. F. Skinner.

10. Speaking of B. F. Skinner, he was born in 1904 in Pennsylvania and is best known for a theory called Behavioral Analysis. He didn't support the idea of free will, but looked at an individual's history more than their anatomy to predict behavior. "Skinner claimed that the mind, or what was then called mentalism, was irrelevant, even nonexistent, and that psychology should only focus on concrete measurable behaviors" (Slater, 2004, p. 6). Skinner's work has been labeled both influential and infamous. "Legend says he built a baby box in which he kept his daughter Deborah for two full years in order to train her, tracking her progress on a grid. The legend also says that when she was thirty-one she sued him for abuse in a genuine court of law, lost the case, and shot herself in a bowling alley in Billings, Montana. None of this is true, and yet the myths persist" (Slater, 2004, p. 7). Wow, what a horrible rumor! If it was true though, maybe that is why he has been quoted as saying, "Give me a child and I'll shape him into anything."

There are many more very well thought of theorists who have contributed to discussions of personality and what it encompasses, and we have given you just a brief overview of some of the commonly encountered theories that were developed early on in the field of psychology. If you found it interesting, you might like to take a psychology course to learn more about the different theories out there. For now however, it's very important to understand the definition of personality, and some of the key theories about personality in order to understand the results from a personality assessment, which is why we've given you a quick little history lesson.

What is a personality assessment? Usually, it's a questionnaire that is put together to try to explain personality traits. Ah, that clears it up completely, right? Okay, there's more to it than that. It would be simple if there was just one personality test you could take to give you all of the answers, but no such luck. It seems like there's someone out there creating a new personality test every day, especially if you're on Facebook! "Which movie star are you?" or "How perverted are you?" Right ... that will tell me a lot about myself! Yeah, those types of surveys don't really pass the validity and reliability test. So, how do you know which ones to take, or which ones are even helpful? That's where the fun begins.

We're now going to discuss some of the most popular and well-regarded tests to explain what they do and why they are important. By understanding each of these tests and what they reveal about people, you'll be able to better understand your friends, family and coworkers. This should help you to avoid beating your head against a wall trying to figure out why they act the way they do.

Personality has a lot to do with human behavior. Anyone who has had more than one baby can probably tell you that personality is there right from the beginning. Two children can be born from the same parents and yet be completely different. We are both personally very aware of that, as there are some questionable characters in our own lineage. Somehow, we managed to dodge a few personality bullets, and fortunately, can function in society to some extent.

Why do people act the way they do? That's a question many psychologists and experts have tried to answer. We're not writing this book to discover "why" people are the way they are. We'll leave that to their underpaid and probably frazzled psychiatrists and psychologists. By the time we meet most of the crazies in the world, including the ones we work with, they already have their established personalities, and there's probably not a lot we can do about it. Why we're writing this book is to explain "what" personalities are all about, and "how" to deal with them, so that you can succeed at work and in life in spite of them. "Your ability to communicate is an important tool in your pursuit of your goals, whether it is with your family, your coworkers, or your clients and customers." Does anyone know who Les Brown is? Never mind. He was responsible for the statement quoted above, and he has a good point. Actually, Les is a well thought of motivational speaker ... we were just testing you. The point is, let's learn how to communicate by understanding the different personalities out there. (I didn't know who he was – but if he is well known then we should act like we know who it is too).

To begin the process, we need to look at personalities, and how we all differ from one another. If you're concerned about nature vs. nurture, there are some parts of personality that can be changed, and others that we're pretty much stuck with. Myers–Briggs is a personality test that we will cover in Chapter 2, but according to the researchers, the results of this test are pretty much set in stone. This test isn't about our personalities per se; rather, it's a test about our preferences for learning. You'll understand soon, we promise;

keep reading. This test is important in understanding where people are coming from, and their results on this test are pretty much about nature. People are born with certain preferences, and they stay that way.

If you look at Emotional Intelligence, however, which we will discuss in Chapter 3, things can be improved. All we can say is, thank God for that! We can think of some emotionally unintelligent people who need help like ... now! Emotional intelligence is about understanding one's emotions, as well as those in others. By being able to develop that understanding, people learn how to communicate and get along with other people better.

Personality tests have been around for a long time, even dating back to Hippocrates. For those of you who didn't do well on history, Hippocrates was a Greek physician who lived around 400 BC. The popularity of personality tests became much more intense after the 20th century, though.

So, how accurate are the results of personality tests? Well, that's debatable. Many would say that the results are subjective. In other words, the results can be hard to measure, and may be subject to people's interpretations or views. Some say that you can give fake answers to skew the results. The most respected tests, however, have gone through reliability and validity testing in an effort to ensure that, hopefully, they are accurate.

Unfortunately, whenever you ask someone to rate themselves on something, they often give you the answer they think you want to hear, or say what they wish they were, rather than what they really are. We all know the jerk who thinks he's so cool and wonderful, while really he's just plain annoying. Some people just don't have a clue. Many of these tests have built in mechanisms that should account and correct for this lack of personal insight and lack of freakin' common sense, though. So, can someone still fake the results on a personality test? Sure, it's still possible. How will that affect us? Probably not so much, because chances are we'll never see the results of their test anyway.

One reason for reading this book is to understand how to spot certain personality traits without forcing your colleague to actually take a test. Later, we'll be discussing the tests so you can understand what they're looking for and how those traits are important in determining why people act the way they do. So, you can throw away all those copies of personality tests you printed off to hand out to your coworkers, because after reading this book, you'll know a lot about their personality simply by interacting with them. Which is a good thing, because we're sure they'd look at you as if you were crazy if you suddenly handed them a personality test. Plus, we don't want you to be a paper waster ... way to go green!

It's important not only to decipher the personality of others, but also to understand your own personality. Judith Martin, the American journalist better known as 'Miss Manners,' was quoted as saying, "It is far more impressive when others discover your good qualities without your help." By understanding behaviors, you can make personal adjustments to learn how best to deal with people and become the superstar at work ... or at least survive another day.

So, what are some examples of personality tests? We're glad you asked. Some of the first tests were used in the early 1900s, but one of the first major tests that you've probably heard of was the Rorschach inkblot test, developed by a guy named Hermann Rorschach. This is the test you see on all the TV shows where the guy looks at a black ink shape on a white card, and it looks like a bat, but the guy feels like he should say it's a butterfly so people don't look at him like he's all Emo or something. Actually, it's interesting that more people do see the bat rather than the butterfly ... or maybe they're just lying. For those of you who saw the movie *Watchmen*, the guy named Rorschach was named after the fact that his face kept changing, like the Rorschach ink-blot test. But you knew that, right?

Anyway, the Rorschach test is basically about having a person look at 10 cards, each with different splotches on them. There's more involved than just looking at the cards, but that's the most interesting part of the test as far as we're concerned. The test taker decides what they think the splotches look like, and the test administrator writes down their descriptions. These comments are supposed to give great insight into the person's personality, motivations, and perceptions.

Here's an oft-cited Rorschach joke: A man goes to see a clinical psychologist. After completing the clinical interview, the clinical psychologist decides that she will administer the Rorschach Inkblot test. The clinical psychologist shows the man the first inkblot and he says he sees a man and a woman making love at the beach. On the second card he sees a man and a woman making love in a hot-tub. On the third, he sees a man and a woman making love in a park. In all of the inkblots, the man sees a couple making love. At the end of the test, the clinical psychologist looks over her notes and says, "You seem to have a preoccupation with sex." The man replies, "You're the one with the dirty pictures"(www.psychinaction.com/uimages//78.doc).

There has been a great deal of controversy over how valid the results from Rorschach's test are. Suffice it to say, the test is considered to be reliable in helping to understand schizophrenia. Hopefully, you don't have a lot of schizos at work, so we won't go into any more detail about this test. However, it is important for you to know what it is so that you don't sound like a total dork for not having heard about it after reading a book about personality assessments.

Another very important personality test was developed by a mother and daughter team, who named it the MBTI. MBTI? What in the world does MBTI stand for? More brilliant than idiotic? Just kidding. It actually has nothing to do with being smart, or stupid, or indeed anything about IQ. It's based on some work originally done by Carl Jung during World War II. MBTI stands for Myers–Briggs Type Indicator, which was developed, interestingly enough, by two people named Myers and Briggs. You can find numerous rip-off versions of this test on the Internet. These are not as valid and reliable as the original test, but they are free, and can give you a rough idea of what the original MBTI would show you. Basically, this test splits people up into 16 different personality types based on how they prefer to process information. If you're so intrigued by this introduction that you can't stand the suspense, check out Chapter 2 for more information on the MBTI.

A very popular term that you'll hear a lot about if you take any business course is the Big Five Factors of Personality. This became really big in the '70s and included the following five parts of one's personality: Openness, Conscientiousness, Extraversion, Agreeableness, and Neuroticism, or OCEAN for short. Two independent research teams came up with the theory that these were the five most important parts of our personality. Some of these traits are also part of the

Emotional Intelligence theory, which we will be covering in Chapter 3. I know, we keep teasing you, and we're sure you're racing to that chapter right now to find out more, but when you come back, we'll continue.

Although the Big Five is a popular model of the important parts of one's personality, we've come up with our own list of five traits you may have seen in some of your coworkers. In our list, the OCEAN acronym stands for Obnoxiousness, Crankiness, Egotism, Annoyance, and Nastiness. For the sake of being politically correct, we'll go with the commonly used factors, though we still like our version better.

It has been argued that these factors are a bit broad in definition, however beneath each of these five factors lie subfactors that go on to explain personality even further. For example, extroversion includes things such as sociability, impulsiveness, excitement, and other emotions.

If you want to identify some of the things that go along with someone's Openness, for example, you might check out their vocabulary, or whether they have a vivid imagination or good ideas. For their Conscientiousness, you'd look to see if they're well prepared, and pay attention to details. Part of their Extraversion includes things like whether they're conversational, and how they act around others. Agreeableness includes their interest in others, and how they understand other people's emotions. Lastly, their Neuroticism is about their general mood, and how easily they get disturbed or annoyed. Researchers have found that all of these factors are pretty close to being determined 50/50 from nature and nurture, or heredity and environment, so at least those people with an annoying personality have a chance at fixing some of it! To learn more about this, check out Chapter 3.

Some correlation between these factors and birth order has also been found. Birth order is often discussed in the media in terms of how it will impact your personality. God forbid you are a middle child! You're just basically out of luck! Or are you? Is it true that firstborns will be the big successes in life? Birth order has come to be considered somewhat of a pop psychology issue, so it's probably best not to worry too much about it.

Remember Alfred Adler? Well, he's the guy who came up with all of this originally. He was around at the time of Jung and Freud, and claimed that firstborns were kicked off their thrones by the second child, and that had a lasting impact. He also claimed that the youngest was usually pampered and spoiled. We're both the youngest child in our respective families, and we have no problem with that. But there was more to Adler's theory than just birth order. There was also consideration given to the gap between siblings. Further, later research showed that gender order had a lot to do with a person's sexual orientation, as well. How does this help you at work? Check out Chapter 4 for more info.

There have been a lot of tests and experiments developed in order to understand why people do the things they do, and some of these tests have shown that people are not easily explainable. A favorite study of ours is the Milgram experiment, which was conducted at Yale in the '60s. This study had a lot to do with the part of people's personality that includes obedience.

Milgram's experiment showed that people would continue to give electric shocks to others based on authority figures telling them it was OK to do so as part of an experiment. Even though there was no real electric shock being given, the subjects of the experiment did not know this, and were willing to shock the heck out of other people because someone in a white lab coat had told them to. What does this tell you about your fellow man? That people will do stupid things just because someone with authority suggests it. This is an important thing to realize in the working world. To borrow a quote from the movie *Men in Black*, "People are dumb, panicky, dangerous animals." By understanding this, we can prepare ourselves to deal with people we are forced to work with who we would normally have the sense to completely ignore in the real world.

Of all of the crazy things people do at work, one of the most frustrating to deal with can be your fellow employee's lack of "Concern for Impact". You're probably now wondering what in the heck that is. Concern for Impact is basically about caring what other people think about you. It has to do with things you say, how you say them, your body language, and your tone. You might be thinking that you have a pretty good idea of what others think about you, and how you're coming across, but you may be very wrong! A lot of how you act and portray yourself is based on how you were raised. Did your mom or dad always act exasperated or annoyed? If so, there's a good chance you might do the same thing and not realize it. Worse still, you might think that it's OK to act like that because that's all you've ever experienced. Maybe you're seen as the complainer or the Debbie Downer of the office, and you don't even know you're seen that way.

The problem at work is, you must be around a lot of other people. Many times, you're assigned to teams where you need to interact with others and not piss them off. You may actually want to move up the corporate ladder and get promoted. Chances are, then, if you don't realize how you come across to others, you may be kidding yourself into thinking you have a better personality than you actually have.

Does that make you stupid? Not necessarily. But having a high IQ may not make you all that wonderful, either. In fact, organizations are now more concerned about your emotional intelligence quotient, or EQ, than your IQ. Why? Just because you're smart doesn't mean you understand how to deal with other people. If you saw the movie A Beautiful Mind starring Russell Crowe, you know that his character was a genius, but had no people skills. He was also completely nuts, but hey ... some of your fellow employees might be as well, although not all people with high IQs are crazy. Whew ... that gets us off the hook. However, just having a high IQ is no guarantee of success.

So, with all of these theories, tests, and ideas about personalities, you may be asking yourself whether you need to take all of these tests to find out more about yourself. Well, you could. A lot of them will probably tell you what you already know deep down inside. What is important to realize is that not all of the tests on the Internet are "quality" tests. A lot of them won't tell you very much at all, in fact many of them are just ways to get you to look at their site so they can sell you something. Some tests, like the actual Myers–Briggs test or one of the well-respected EQ tests might be helpful in giving you some insight into who you are, but with or without those results, the most important thing is that you understand not only what your results mean, but also what other people's results mean for you.

Again, that doesn't mean you need to get everyone at work to take a personality test just so you can understand them better, which is not to say it hasn't been done. Diane worked at an office where the Management by Strengths

(MBS) test was given to all employees, and everyone's results were actually posted on the wall of their cubicle for others to observe and respond to accordingly. The MBS test assigns people to different color groups such as Blue, Green, Red, or Yellow. The thought process behind having everyone display their color (both of us are Green, by the way) was that others would know how to respond to them. For example, a Blue likes to have a little extra time to complete activities. They don't like to be rushed. By knowing this about your co-worker, you would be less likely to slam something on their desk while yelling that you wanted it yesterday. We keep foreshadowing what is to come later on in the book, but if you really want to find out more about color personality tests, check out Chapter 7.

In the real world, most people don't walk around with a sign on their forehead, although we sometimes think Bill Ingvall has a point in his quest to have people wear a sign on their heads to let us know they're stupid. In his famous routine, he said:

> *"I just hate stupid people. They should have to wear signs that just say 'I'm stupid.' That way you wouldn't rely on them, would you? You wouldn't ask them anything. It would be like, "Excuse me ... oops, never mind. I didn't see your sign."*

Our hope in writing this book is to teach you how to figure out what people's signs should say on their forehead. We're sure plenty of them will have the 'stupid' sign, in addition to their other personality signs, but in the rest of this book, we'll try to explain what those personality signs are all about, and how to deal with them so that you make it through your workday with a little less frustration.

Think of it as being like you are able to read people's minds, kind of like Mel Gibson in *What Women Want*. In the movie, he had no clue what people were really thinking about him until he got electrocuted and could hear women's thoughts. The good news here is, you won't actually have to be electrocuted. You'll be able to figure out not just women's personalities, but men's as well, and you'll also be able to sleep at night without hearing voices in your head.

In the working world, think of the advantage you would have if you could understand why people act the way they do, and could play on that. You could get along with even the most annoying of characters. You could play the "get promoted" game, because you'd have insight into what people really wanted. You wouldn't have to guess why people weren't responding to you, or try to come up with ideas that were never going to fly in the first place. Think of all the time you're currently wasting being frustrated by people. By understanding yourself and others, your job could actually become something you enjoy doing.

CHAPTER 1:
THE YOUNG ADULT

"An individual's self-concept is the core of his personality.
It affects every aspect of human behavior: the ability
to learn, the capacity to grow and change.
A strong, positive self-image is the best possible
preparation for success in life."

— Dr. Joyce Brothers

We wrote this book for young adults and for those who want to understand young adults. Therefore, we thought it would be appropriate to include a chapter in which we define what we mean by the phrase "young adults", and also provide some background on some of the issues that are facing this group of people. Here, we're going to be discussing some of the issues and misconceptions associated with people who are of high-school age through to their mid-30s. As we stated earlier, we're simply going to give these young people the collective label of NewGens, to make things easier to follow.

This group has contained many stereotypes over the years. Abma (2009) claims that Generation X has been "classified as being cynical, independent and sensitive to what they see as attempts by others to micromanage them. Gen Y are often seen by older coworkers as lazy, difficult to manage and prepared to abandon their companies in an instant for other opportunities." A study released by the Conference Board of Canada showed that there were actually many similarities between these groups and other generations in terms of personality types. Studies are showing that different generations may have the same objectives at work, as well.

Part of the bad rap that younger generations are receiving is due to some of the work done by Twenge et al. (2008), which claims that younger generations have more issues with self-esteem and narcissism. Having narcissism or being narcissistic means you are overly concerned with "you". Basically, you're in love with yourself. This is not a good thing, as it leads to having overly high expectations and a feeling that you deserve only the best and should not have to work hard to get it. It has been suggested that this is damaging to companies who hire this group of people. If young adults feel that they should win, no matter what the cost, this can also lead to ethical issues in the workplace. We'll talk about narcissism in more depth later.

It has been suggested that the changing family unit is part of what makes the newer generations different. With over half of the families out there consisting of divorced parents, children often receive more focus than with previous generations. According to scribd.com, "Over half of families with children eat dinner together seven days a week. The dinner setting gives parents and children time to discuss important events."

Technology has also had a strong impact on this generation. Those who are entering the workforce now will have a much stronger technological background than their predecessors. Although employers have complained that new entrants into job positions expect a high income immediately, this group is not averse to some hard work, however they may jump around a bit, and not necessarily stay in a job for 20–30 years like previous generations. In fact, many say they would eventually like to end up self-employed.

According to birdkman.com, there are some important perks when considering hiring Millennials, including the fact that they respond well to feedback, they accept responsibility, and they're used to teamwork. Leaders just need to remember that this group likes flexibility in order to stay motivated. Sharon Fink, from ManageSmarter, claims that, "for Millennials, everything is about speed, customization, and interactivity – the more digital the better. ... Millennials expect consistent and positive feedback. Perhaps the members of no other generation have bonded so closely with their peers (as much through technology as through personal interaction), and their emphasis on collaboration combines with skill at multitasking to give them more friends than members of other generations can possibly imagine." That isn't to say they don't come with issues. Richard Sweeney's work (2006) showed that they can be a very impatient group, requiring constant feedback and instant gratification. Further, they haven't been inclined to educate themselves through reading newspapers or other literature. Sweeney's work concluded that this may lead to a decline in their writing skills.

Although this book combines Gen X and Gen Y/Millennials in terms of the intended audience, there are in fact some differences between these groups. According to Newstrategist.com, "The Millennials are the first generation born into the high-tech world. They are growing up with computers and the Internet, with cell phones and genetic engineering. Unlike older generations, which have had to struggle to adapt, most Millennials are sailing effortlessly into the high-tech 21st century. The future belongs to them." This group is younger than their predecessors, the Gen X group, who Newstrategist.com refers to as a "well-educated, media-savvy generation . . . who face the same problems that confronted Boomers – a conflict between work and family roles."

Generation X and Millennials include nearly as many heads of households as the past Baby Boomer generation. As these two groups have come to make up a larger portion of the population, it has lead to the workplace becoming less formal and more relaxed. If you work somewhere that has casual Fridays, it's probably due to this influence. Twenge and Campbell (2008) had some positive things to say about young adults. They claimed that "today's employees are prepared to take greater risks and are encouraged and rewarded for thinking outside of the box rather than sticking to the traditional ways of doing things." This can be advantageous, because it steers the organization away from group-think and promotes more of an entrepreneurial atmosphere.

There has also been some concern about the younger generations becoming more and more depressed and filled with anxiety. Twenge and Campbell claim that "Only 1 to 2 percent of Americans born before 1915 experienced a major depressive episode during their lifetimes, even though they lived through the Great Depression and two World Wars. In one 1990s study, 21 percent of teens aged 15 to 17 had already experienced major depression. Anxiety increased so much that the average college student in the 1990s was more anxious than 85 percent of students in the 1950s and 71 percent of students in the 1970s." I guess that's good news for the makers of Xanax and Prozac, but if you're in that group of students, it's not so good.

Some say that the 'Gen' labels are just that – labels, and not a real indicator of personalities. Is all of the hype about the young adult generation just based upon myths? Are those in these generations "edgy" as Hollywood or the media would have you believe? It seems like every definition of Gen X or Gen Y is a little different. Robinson (2006) claims that some people see Gen X as a "classic unsupervised generation – the latchkey kids who mothers poured into the workplace" and Gen Y as those who "grew up on near-constant parenting, counseling, teaching and coaching that emphasized self-esteem."

Robinson also says that according to consulting firm Rain Maker Thinking in New Haven, Connecticut, "Today, generations X and Y – the roughly 120 million people born between 1965 and 1989 – make up 51 percent of the work force. That is a substantial number of people in the workforce who could probably use a better understanding of their personalities and how this understanding could help them work better together."

One of the main issues that comes up a lot specifically with the Gen Y generation is that they expect to be told how wonderful they are all the time. Come on, get over yourselves already! If you're always being told you're a winner, how do you handle it when you get out into the real world where not everyone can be a winner?

Organizations are finding that they have to adjust their management and leadership styles to meet the unusual expectations of the younger generation. Apparently, this generation is stuck in the elementary school "make you feel good" rating system, where more than likely you'll always get an "A" for effort, or a gold star just for showing up and participating. Time to grow up! It's the working world now, and we can guarantee your boss isn't going to be handing out gold stars every time you simply do what is expected of you.

Robert Half International, a large consulting and staffing firm, has created a very helpful brochure explaining what Millennials expect on the job. Check out http://www.rhi.com/GenY. Here are some of the things they have found about Millennials.

Millennials' Dress Preference:

Business casual	**41%**
Sneakers and jeans	**27%**
A mix, or it depends	**26%**
Business attire	**4%**

Also from Half, Millennials discussed their job considerations on a scale of 1–10 scale in terms of what is important to them, where 1 is least important and 10 most important:

Salary	**9.05**
Benefits	**8.86**
Opportunity for growth	**8.74**
Company location	**8.44**
Company leadership	**7.95**
Company/brand reputation	**7.56**

Job title	**7.19**
In-house training	**6.95**
Tuition reimbursement	**6.44**
Diversity of staff	**6.07**
Charitable efforts	**6.06**

As far as work environments go, Millennials ranked what they found important, again on a scale of 1–10, with 1 being least important and 10 the most important:

Working with respected manager	**8.74**
Working with people I enjoy	**8.69**
Having work/life balance	**8.63**
Having a short commute	**7.55**
Working for a responsible company	**7.42**
Having a nice office space	**7.14**
Working with top technology	**6.89**

Employers are realizing that with Baby Boomers now retiring, they are going to have to learn how to understand Millennials more than ever before. Companies are changing their training programs to better meet the needs of this unique group. Bnet.com (2009) claims that "UPS has begun to abandon its training manuals for hands-on learning in staged neighborhoods; Deloitte empowers its middle managers to offer flexible scheduling to their team members, and Google bypasses corporate hierarchy by making its brightest new Millennials managers and granting them direct access to the company's co-founders."

Many interesting terms have been coined in relation to the Generation Y or Millennial group. Generation Y has sometimes been called 'Generation Why,' due to their seemingly endless curiosity. They've also been labeled quick learners, and can be very motivated under the right circumstances. They can also strive to succeed based on their need to please. The term 'Trophy Children' refers to the fact that they have a strong desire to please their parents and give them reason to brag about them. Parents of this new generation have kept very close to their children, even after graduation, indeed many Millennials have been known to move back in with their parents after initially leaving the nest, something that has been termed 'Boomeranging.'

Some typical characteristics of the Gen Y group, according to Lifescript.com (2009), are:

- Family ties – they may move back home after moving out to save money. This is seen as a smart move.
- Tech savvy – they have an advantage over even the Gen X group.
- Short attention spans – they're good multi-taskers, but may get bored easily.
- Social values – they're family people, like diversity at work, and are environmentally conscious.
- Use of free time – they like to study overseas, prefer exploring and discovering, and are productive.
- Compliant – they may be willing to volunteer.

- Outspoken – they don't see being outspoken as being rude, in fact they like to question the status quo.

Harvard Business Publishing (2009) author Tammy Erickson claims that Gen X has the leaders we need right now. Some of the characteristics she claims Gen X has include:

- Resourcefulness – due to being latch-key kids.
- Self-reliance – due to distrust of institutions.
- Adopters – due to a sense of alienation, and having to accept technology.
- Multicultural – due to growing up with so many global issues.
- Innovative – due to preferring alternative ways, which leads to entrepreneurial achievements.
- Practical – due to being skeptical.
- Having work/life balance understanding – due to having dedicated parents.
- Pragmatic – due to having practical and value-oriented sensibilities.

There have been many studies that have looked at how age/generations affect experiences in the workplace. Whether you are looking at Gen X or Gen Y/Millennials, there are some differences between these groups. The Sloan Center on Aging & Work at Boston College (2009) found the following in their study among employees of different age groups:

"- Millennials/Generation Y'ers (ages 26 or younger) had significantly lower work overload (were less overloaded by their work) scores than Generation X'ers (ages 27 to 42) and Baby Boomers (ages 43 to 61).
- Millennials/Generation Y'ers (ages 26 or younger) and the younger Generation X'ers (ages 27 to 35) were less likely to say that their work is full of meaning and

purpose than Baby Boomers (ages 43 to 61) and the Traditionalists/Silent Generation (ages 62 or older).

- Millennials/Generation Y'ers (ages 26 or younger) reported greater opportunities for learning and development compared to older Generation X'ers (ages 36 to 42)."

With all of this data, sometimes telling us conflicting things about these generations, how do we know how to communicate with one another well? Some claim that these generations are no different from any other in the fact that we have to understand each person on an individual level. It may seem simple to categorize everyone into age groups, and claim that because they are Gen X or Gen Y they will act in a certain way, but they are, in fact, like any other generation of people, each of whom have unique personalities that are based on their individual experiences. What we can do, however, is learn to understand personalities and personality assessments so that we can appreciate a diverse group of people, no matter what their age. What a perfect time to jump into our first personality assessment, Myers–Briggs.

CHAPTER 2:
MYERS-BRIGGS

"Personality has the power to open many doors, but character must keep them open."

— Anonymous

We've all worked with people we find annoying, or not terribly bright, even. Some people just take forever to spit out what they want to say, while others never shut up. Some are so unbelievably sensitive, while others seem to have a heart of stone. Sometimes, it would be nice to be able to just go to work and not have to deal with all the crazies out there. Unfortunately, we have to learn to play nice in the working world.

Have you ever thought it would be wonderful to have a manual with explanations of why people act so annoying? Well, here it is. Everyone is born with a unique personality type. In case you've been living under a rock, and weren't paying attention earlier, there's a test out there that a lot of people take called the Myers–Briggs assessment. This is a fun little personality test whose results explain why people have preferences for doing things certain ways. So, stop using Wedding Crasher's "Rule #5: You're an idiot" as your classification system at work, learn the Myers–Briggs assessment instead, and USE IT!

Myers and Briggs were a mother and daughter team, just like us. Well, maybe not as cool as us, but they worked together just like us, and expanded on some work by Carl Jung. You'll recall we talked about Carl Jung in the first chapter; he's like a Freud kind of guy, and dealt with psychobabble while explaining experience and emotions. He died in 1961, but prior to that, he was a pretty smart psychiatrist dude who had some neat ideas about personality assessment, but Myers and Briggs took the ball and ran with it from there. We women are smart that way!

Katharine Briggs and her daughter Isabel Briggs Myers took Jung's types and revelations about people's personalities and developed a test. Who gets a gold star for remembering what MBTI stands for?! Yep, well done ... the Myers–Briggs Type Indicator (MBTI), which was published in 1962 and is one of the most popular, and most studied, tests around. You can take the test yourself, to see what your MBTI is, at www.MyersBriggs.org. If you take it, just make sure you give quick answers. If you think about it for too long, it's not as effective. So, if you don't already know your MBTI result, will you just take it already?! But really, test yourself first, before you read much further, so you'll understand what the heck we're talking about.

We know what you're thinking ... a test? No thanks! But don't give it a thumbs down just yet. Why should you take it? Because it tells you cool stuff about yourself and about other people. Don't get nervous, because it's not testing your IQ or asking in-depth questions. It's more like a questionnaire that will tell you which type of brain you have.

You mean not all brains are the same? Well, not exactly! According to the Myers–Briggs assessment, there are 16 different types of brains out there, 17 if you count that scary dude that asked us for change this morning, but never mind him. Your brain is categorized based on your preferences for learning and tendencies to act a certain way. Plus, many organizations today are testing their employees, so you can find out what they'll be learning about you should you find yourself being tested. Organizations like to use the MBTI instrument to improve employee communication, teamwork, and leadership, and mostly to give you a clear understanding of yourself and others to create greater impact on your daily interactions in the workplace. In other words, you can learn how to interact with that irritating co-worker you can't stand if you know what type of personality they have. Carl Jung himself said it best: "Everything that irritates us about others can lead us to an understanding of ourselves."

What the MBTI doesn't tell you is how smart you are, or whether you're mature or not. That's too bad, because we're sure you can think of a few people who need to measure their levels there. What it does do, however, is break your personal preferences down into 4 areas, which will decide whether you are an introvert or an extrovert, sensing or intuitive, thinking or feeling, judging or perceptive. Yeah, we know. They're a bunch of big words that sound technical, but they're actually really interesting. Think of each area or preference almost like being right-handed or left-handed. Most people are either one way or the other. You might be able to use both, but you're more comfortable with one over the other, right, unless you're a freak! So, read on, and you may learn a little bit about yourself, come to understand other people a little better, and possibly learn how to interact in situations without driving yourself and others freaking crazy.

The chart below provides a quick explanation of the difference preferences associated with the MBTI. Now we'll explain each preference in more detail.

Description		
How people derive "energy"	**Extroversion**	Introversion
How people gather "information", i.e. perceive	**Sensing**	Intuition
How people make "decisions", i.e. judge	**Feeling**	Thinking
Determination if people have a preference for judging or perceiving	**Judging**	**Perceiving**

Introvert vs. Extrovert

You've probably heard the first two terms: Introvert and Extrovert. In fact, you may have seen Extrovert written as Extravert in some places. Myers–Briggs lists Extravert, while many other sites refer to the similar quality as Extrovert. For continuity, we will use Extrovert here. A lot of people just assume that Introverts are quiet nerds, suffering from chronic lonesomeness, while Extroverts don't know how to shut their mouth, but that's not necessarily the case. It's more about where you get your energy from, and we're not talking about Red Bull here. Allow us to explain. There are two different ways of focusing your attention. During various events in our daily lives, we tend to utilize both Introversion and Extroversion, but most people have a dominant expression of one of the two. Here we go with that right-handed, left-handed stuff again! If you don't know whether you're Introverted or Extroverted, put yourself in the two situations below to determine your frame of mind in each. (Note: Do not base your decision on what type you are after a few drinks, because most people turn into an Extrovert when alcohol is added to the mix.)

Situation #1: Have you ever been talking to someone and you asked him or her a question and they just gave you that 'deer in the headlights' look, a 'light's on, but no one's home' kind of look, but didn't answer you? Did you feel a need to end their sentences for them? Did it drive you crazy that it took them so long to respond? Or did you feel like they were giving you the silent treatment? Then you're probably an Extrovert, and you were talking to an Introvert.

Situation #2: Have you ever been in a conversation where the person you were talking to wouldn't shut up, and just seemed to blab blab blab everything they were thinking without any filters? Or they kept firing questions at you and never gave you any time to answer? You start visualizing the duct tape over their mouth, right? If you felt that way, you're probably an Introvert who was talking to an Extrovert.

Which one is it better to be? Although we'd like to say Extrovert, because that's what we are, there's really no "right" way to be. It's just that Extroverts are energized by those things in the outside world, whereas Introverts are energized by those things in the inner world. But what the heck does that mean? Basically, Extroverts do their thinking by talking, and feed off social interaction with others, whereas Introverts are energized by their own thoughts and personal space, and tend to become drained by social scenes.

Believe it or not, 60–75% of the U.S. population are Extroverts. If you're an Extrovert, you're probably as sociable as Jim Carrey on cocaine. Okay, that's a bit of an exaggeration, but sometimes, that's how Introverts feel about all us Extroverts. If you've been called a "social butterfly" a time or two, you might consider yourself an Extrovert. Typically, an Extrovert tends to talk first, gives their opinion a lot, loves to be in the limelight and is very approachable, but also needs affirmation from others around them.

Introverts are definitely out-numbered in this Extroverted society of ours, and are sometimes seen as being unfriendly and otherwise unapproachable. Let's not stereotype here, though, because not all Introverts are shy and lack social skills; they simply have different social needs, preferences, and ways of thinking. Introverts have unique strengths, and should be just as socially acceptable as Extroverts, indeed Introverts would say even more so, because these types of people are great listeners, enjoy having time to themselves to relax and recharge their batteries, and are usually reserved and reflective. Introverts prefer not to rush things, and have high concentration levels.

You've probably heard the famous quote, "The less you speak the more you will hear." This is the epitome of an introverted statement. Some Introverted people may become so wrapped up in their own inner world that others might not understand them, because they haven't communicated their thoughts and/or preferences. This may cause Introverts to withdraw further into themselves, because they then assume that others don't understand or appreciate them.

Why in the world should you care if someone is Introverted or Extroverted? Because when drama occurs in the workplace, understanding the differences between the two and their communication styles makes it easier to effectively address and solve the issues.

For example, let's say you're an Extrovert who has to work with an Introvert. You ask them a question, and it takes them FOREVER, okay, 5 seconds, to respond. What does that do to you, the Extrovert? It makes you want to shoot somebody! You're thinking, "What the heck is the matter with this guy?" You want to scream, "I don't think you're appreciating the urgency here; I asked you a question." Why hasn't he freakin' answered?! What do you do about it? You answer for him. Why? Because you assume he doesn't know the answer. Wrong! That assumption is incorrect. Chill out; be patient. He's just processing what he wants to say to you. By answering your own questions and ending his sentences, you're just pissing him off and being insensitive to his particular way of processing information.

Here's why understanding Myers–Briggs is important. If you know that the person you're talking to is an Introvert, you can tell yourself internally that this guy isn't an idiot; he's just processing. He knows what you asked him, and now he's just developing a good answer in his head. He's not ignoring you; he just isn't babbling out loud like you would. By realizing that this horrific 5-second delay is okay, you're no longer frustrated; you can wait. And you can now make sense of the silence.

You're probably wondering, is everyone either an Extrovert or an Introvert? Good question grasshopper! The answer is no. You could have a strong preference one way or the other, or you could go both ways at various times.

If you haven't taken the Myers–Briggs test yet, ask yourself a couple of questions to see which way you think you lean. Do you like to come up with your answers by speaking your thoughts out loud, or do you prefer to think internally? Do you like to be around people, or do you prefer to be alone? Are you relaxed and confident, or reserved and questioning? If you answered yes to the first part of these questions and no to the second part, you're probably more of an Extrovert. If it was the other way around, then you're probably an Introvert. Depending on your mood or situation, you may answer these questions differently on occasion, but more than likely, you'll generally lean to one side or the other.

What is interesting about these personality types is that you are basically born this way. You can take the test today, and then if you take it again years from now, the results will probably be pretty similar. Yep, that's right ... if you don't like your personality, sorry, but you're kind of stuck with it! It's all about the preferences that we're born with. You might be able to be outgoing and talkative under the right conditions, but in general, you may prefer not to be.

Sometimes, it's hard to know if someone is Introverted or Extroverted. People tend to try to be more Extroverted in the workplace, but may actually be Introverted at home. Some Introverts can come out of their shell and act differently in different contexts; take actors and comedians for example. Their job is to be entertaining, so it seems to be a requirement to be Extroverted.

Would you ever have thought that comedian Chris Rock or actor Will Ferrell are Introverts? Well, it's said that they are, or at least more shy than you would anticipate, in real life. Professional comedians are shyer than most other people. "I guess the stage gives them the opportunity to be what they want to be and may not necessarily represent their daily-life personalities," says Gil Greengross, an anthropologist at the University of New Mexico in Albuquerque. "The fact is that a lot of the time they spend by themselves. They also travel a lot. That might explain why they do have introverted personalities," Greengross adds.

Just as comedians or actors may seem Extroverted because they perform that way while "working the stage," many Introverts do the same at work, but in reality might actually be more reserved than you think. Does that mean that everyone needs to "act" Extroverted at work? No, but these days there is a greater reliance on team-based activities in the workplace, and therefore higher social interaction requirements. Therefore, the functional differences between Introverts and Extroverts tend to create specialization in the workplace. Typically, Introverts and Extroverts are often driven to different careers. Even so, both types are more than likely going to have to work together at some point, so it's very important to recognize the differing personality types to decrease the gap in communication and minimize the drama. Nobody likes drama! So, if you're an Introvert, you may have to step up your social skills a little more if you have to work in teams. When we discuss personality assessments shortly, we'll suggest some different career paths that might be more suitable for all you mellow people if it's too difficult to fake the high-energy personality.

Extroverts Test Yourself: If you're an Extrovert, next time you have a conversation at work with someone, try asking them questions ... give someone else a chance for a change, would you! Ask them about their families, or what they did over the weekend. Even though you probably don't care, you might actually end up making a new friend, and Extroverts LOVE friends! It won't kill you! Try to show that you care about someone other than yourself. You may be sick of hearing the expression, "You have two ears and one mouth so you should listen twice as much as you talk", but there's something to it.

Learning how to listen is an important step to becoming good at sales, management, or just about any job that involves people, which is most jobs, really. Stop being so focused on your own life and think about someone else for a change. You might be surprised at how much you learn from listening to others. It will drive you nuts at first, and you'll be just dying to state your point. You might even be thinking about what you want to say, instead of listening to what the other guy is saying, but lock it up; your ADHD excuse doesn't work anymore! Shut up and really listen to what comes out of the other guy's mouth. If more Extroverts took time to do this, they might have more appreciation for the input of others.

Want to know how to spot an Extrovert or an Introvert during communication?

Extrovert	**Introvert**
Talks Fast	May be slow to answer
Interrupts others	Low volume voice
Thinks out loud	Thinks internally

Introverts Test Yourself: Next time you're having a conversation at work with an Extrovert, before you take your time thinking about what you're going to say, try prefacing your comment with something like, "That's a good question ... give me a minute to think about a good answer." If you let them know you got their Q, and are working on their A, the Extrovert knows you're actually doing something, instead of just sitting there staring at him with a dumb expression on your face. If you give an Extrovert something, anything, other than dead air, they at least know you heard them. The most painful thing to an Extrovert is waiting for a response. Giving them a short, interim response like that means they are more likely to be patient.

So, now that you understand and appreciate the differences between Extroverts and Introverts, here comes the next area of personality differences.

Sensing vs. Intuition

Okay, now that you could pretty much teach a class on being Introverted or Extroverted, try your hand at understanding why some people prefer Sensing, and others prefer Intuition. Pay attention though, because it's said that the differences between these two preferences are the most pronounced of the four areas. However, if the two can learn to work together, a powerful team results. So, if you can learn to work with the opposite preference, well ... then, of course, you can challenge the Klingons for interstellar domination.

Hold on, though; first you need to know how the two areas prefer to perceive information before getting to that level. So, you have your Sensors. Does that mean you sniff out information? Well, kind of ... but don't get ahead of yourself, Sherlock Holmes. Sensors like to deal with information through the use of the five senses, seeing, hearing, tasting, touching and smelling. Then, you have your Intuitives. Does that mean they have ESP? Not exactly. Intuitives prefer to deal with information by using their sixth sense; feeling, or intuition. This isn't an "I see dead people" kind of sense, but more of a "gut feeling" that is used when processing information.

Sensors like to rely on facts and figures. Nerd alert! Oops, wait ... that's what Diane does. Just like Extroverts, the majority of the population tends to be Sensors, rather than Intuitives. Sensors, who we will refer to as the S's, like details and facts before they make decisions. They're very practical, hands-on people who live for the present moment. You don't have to be an accountant or a lawyer to prefer to use your senses, but you may be drawn to jobs where you get to work with details and numbers. A lot of Sensors become experts in their field. If you've watched *The Office*, Dwight would definitely be a Sensor. But don't stereotype S's simply based on our use of Dwight as an example. Just because S's tend to live a repetitive, grounded lifestyle doesn't mean they're boring people who are destined to work in a cubicle! They're also 'here and now' kinds of people.

In contrast, Intuitives, or the N's, look for patterns, and how things relate to each other. N's live in the world of ideas, and think in terms of future potential. They love change, and are all about anticipating the future; they're always thinking about what exciting thing will come next. Sometimes, they don't seem like they are paying attention because they are off playing around in their head, thinking of possibilities. N's can be great innovators, because they tend to think of things no one else has ever thought of before. To keep an Intuitive happy at work, it's important to mix things up and make sure that things are always new and changing. Data entry would definitely not be a good job choice for these guys!

Which way is better to be; an S or an N? Again, put your swords away. It's no better being one or the other. Diane is totally a Sensor, but Toni tends be in the middle in this category, with some of the preferences of both S's and N's. So, not only is it no better to be distinctly one way or the other, but you can have a little bit of the preferences of both.

Why is this category said to be the most important? Well, it helps to know where people stand in this category at work because teams work better if you have a combination of personality types. If everyone on a team was Intuitive, there may be too much thinking about the future and not enough doing things in the present moment. On the other hand, if everyone was a Sensor, there may not be as much creativity. By combining different personalities into teams, they become much more effective.

Ask yourself this ... do you have to read a textbook beginning from page one and proceeding to page two, then to page three and so on and never skip around? If so, you may be a Sensor. Do you tend to jump around within the book to check out what different chapters have to offer? Then you may be an Intuitive. Many engineers and CPAs are S's, while artistic types tend to be more N's. It's all about attention to detail.

Want to know how to spot a Sensor or Intuitive during communication?

Sensor	**Intuitive**
Wants instructions	Wants to know purpose
Asks a lot of questions	Wants to know possibilities
Wants precision	Likes generality of terms

Test Yourself: When we were training organizations about the importance of Myers–Briggs, we liked to do a fun little game. First, we split the people up into two groups. One group was all Sensors, while the other group was all Intuitives. Then, we gave each group a box of Legos and told them to build something. They were given about 20 minutes to design and come up with their "something", and neither group could see what the other group was building. The Sensing group came up with a very simple design that was good, but wasn't particularly unusual. The N's also came up with a good design, but theirs was more creative and unusual. Think about what you would build if you were given this activity.

Now, let's apply this example to activities in the workplace. The N's want to create new ideas and provide a better solution with their creations, whereas the S's are keen to gather the details and components necessary to bring the idea into reality. Both are very important and needed aspects in the workplace. As we stated previously, if the S's and N's are capable of working together, a very successful team can result.

By now, you should know whether you're an Introvert or an Extrovert, whether you prefer Sensing or Intuition, and the differences between these areas. Congratulations! You're now half way towards becoming a MBTI expert and ultimately getting along with everyone in the workplace. Give yourself a pat on the back!

The next preference area can create lots of conflicts if it isn't approached correctly, so let's dip in to the next section and find out whether you use more emotions or more logic when making decisions.

Thinking vs. Feeling

Do you use reason or emotion to approach a decision? What part of our personality influences that? This is where the Thinking and Feeling functions come in. A Thinking person is pretty self-explanatory. These people use logic, and are objective when making decisions. They like rules and procedures. Everything is pretty much black or white to the Thinking group, and there isn't a lot of room for interpretation. It's either pass or fail, go or stop. Basically, it's Diane to a "T." If your boss is a Thinker and you turn in a proposal that contains an error, the first thing he's likely to say is that you made a mistake, without stopping to think about your feelings. He's being impersonal, but don't worry, he's not purposely trying to hurt your feelings.

A Feeling person is also pretty much like the term sounds. They decide things based on their values and perceptions, basing their decisions on how the outcome will affect them. Will it hurt their feelings? Will it make them happy or sad? For them, it's all largely based on their value system and personal concerns. If your boss is a Feeling person and you turn in your proposal with an error, the first thing he might say is thank you, because he would appreciate your effort. Only then would he be likely to notice the error.

Interestingly, Diane came up with the strongest preference you can have for being a Thinker rather than a Feeler. Does that make her out to be cold or mean? No, it just means she's very logical. Toni came out as a stronger Feeler. Does that make her overly sensitive and emotional? No, it just means she makes decisions by weighing what people care about, and taking into account the points of view of the people involved in a situation. If you came out as high as Toni on the feeling scale, you care about the feelings of others. You might even bake cookies for people to show you care. Diane doesn't bake many cookies, so does that mean she doesn't care? No, it just means she puts more emphasis on utilizing logic to find answers to things. The person who bakes the cookies may be working on reaching someone through doing something that they value themselves; they would probably love to receive cookies themselves.

The funny thing is, the Feeling person who makes the cookies for the Thinking person may be wasting their time, because the Thinking person may not see the value of the cookies.

Meanwhile, the Feeling person thinks that the person they are giving the cookies to should be appreciating them as much as they enjoyed making them. Unfortunately, feelings sometimes get hurt when these two types don't realize how the other type feels. A Feeling person giving another Feeling person cookies = happiness for both parties. A Feeling person giving a Thinking person cookies = possible dissatisfaction for one party, because they may feel like they should reciprocate, when it's not really their style.

It's easy to stereotype these two preferences. Being a Feeler doesn't mean you carry tissues around everywhere you go and cry like Lloyd and Harry in *Dumb and Dumber* while watching a phone company commercial or Brendan Frazier sniveling in *Bedazzled*, but if someone appears to be friendlier than most, treating people uniquely, they're probably more of a Feeling person. Likewise, Thinkers aren't all cold-hearted, overly insensitive Ari Gold from *Entourage* types, but if someone appears to be more business-like in nature, they're probably a Thinker. It's important to understand these differences at work, especially if you're working in teams containing different types of people. The Thinker may be a good one to assign to analyzing plans, whereas the Feeler may be better suited to understanding people and what motivates them.

On the negative side, sometimes Thinkers may come across as cold and condescending toward Feelers, while Feelers may come across as too emotional to the Thinkers. What's important is to realize that we're born this way, and we all have important things to offer. By understanding these differences, we can be more patient toward and understanding of the other guy.

Want to know how to spot a Thinker vs. a Feeler during communication?

Thinker	Feeler
Tests you with questions	Looks for harmony
Weighs evidence	Talks values
Right vs. wrong	Good vs. bad
Not impressed with others' reaction	Interested in how others react
Communication flows logically	Wants others' opinions to be considered

Test Yourself: Is it true or valid? Or is it important to me? If you approach your decision-making process with the first question, you're a Thinker. You're a Feeler if you ask yourself the second question when making a decision.

Again, each person is capable of making both Thinking and Feeling decisions, but the MBTI scale determines what type of decisions you prefer. Once you determine your decision-making preference, you'll have a better idea of what sort of work you prefer to do. Typically, Thinkers prefer a work environment that will allow them to utilize their analytical and logical skills, whereas Feelers like to use their warm and caring attributes on a more personal work level to create a positive impact and feel appreciated in what they do. Realistically, however, there will be both Thinkers and Feelers in every work environment. So, now that you know the differences between the two preferences, you can learn how to cancel out the bad chemistry and adapt to the way your opposite type makes decisions. Okay, there's one more preference area to go ... you're almost there!

Judging vs. Perceptive

The last two parts of the personality puzzle are the terms Judging and Perceptive. These two preferences describe a person's overall lifestyle. Don't mistake Judging as being

Judgmental. Rather, think of Judging as having a plan. Those who are Judging are probably going to make their flight on time. They live by a schedule, and are extremely organized and prepared. The Perceptive person, on the other hand, is more of a 'fly by the seat of their pants' kind of person. If they miss that flight, they know another one will eventually come along. The Perceptive person takes life as it comes, and is more flexible and impulsive. However, these two types can drive each other crazy. If you're a Judging person, it's important to understand that the Perceptive person likes the thrill of surprise. If you're a Perceptive person, it's important to understand that the Judging person may not want to be surprised.

You've probably seen the guy who has "to do" lists everywhere. That guy is a Judging person. He likes routines, and enjoys checking things off his list as he completes them. To a Perceptive person, however, making a "to do" list is about as useful as tits on a bull. It's just not that important to them. Understandably, there can be tension if these two types are working together. The Judging person may have a timeframe in mind that he really wants to meet, while the Perceptive person may think it's more important to be flexible and keep their minds open for some last minute ideas to pop up. A Perceptive person works better close to the deadline, with a mentality of "the sooner you fall behind, the more time you'll have to catch," whereas a Judging person wants to keep ahead of deadlines, and isn't as tolerant of time pressure. A Judging person likes to make the decision and move on, while the Perceptive person likes to keep their options open.

You might consider the Judging person to be a control freak. They want to know what is going to happen next, and when. Conversely, you might consider the Perceptive person as a "go with the flow" kind of guy. If you're going to be throwing a surprise party, better to do it for the Perceptive person rather than the Judging person. Diane's husband has more of a Judging personality, and is still freaked out by the surprise party she threw for him six years ago. She should have heeded her own advice and not put him through that.

Judging people like routines, and like to do the same thing the same way most of the time. They enjoy knowing the answer to a question. If you've ever watched *Friends*, Monica is definitely a Judging person. On the other hand, the Perceptive person has fun learning how to do the same thing in different ways. On *Friends*, that would definitely be Phoebe!

Other good examples involving television characters are Eric "E" Murphy and Vincent Chase from *Entourage*. Vince is impulsive, spends money that he doesn't have, is a procrastinator, never reads his scripts when told, often shows up late, is spontaneous, and takes risks, whereas "E," Vince's manager, is structured, timely, and responsible.

Think about how people handle deadlines at work. The Judging person hears that the work assignment is due on Friday. To him, that means that he starts right now, and doesn't stop until it is finished. To the Perceptive person, they have until Friday, so they figure out in their mind how much time it will take them, and only worry about starting it when that time is near. So if they decide it will take them one day, they may not start working on it until Thursday. Waiting like this would destroy the Judging person, but the Perceptive person doesn't see a problem with it. What is important for the Judging person to know at work is that just because the Perceptive person isn't yet working on a project, they'll manage to finish it on time, as long as they're given a deadline.

In college, did you ever pull an all-nighter? If so, you're probably not the Judging kind of person. Toni pulled many all-nighters, especially during her Senioritis phase. The Judging person (ahem, that would be Diane) probably has no idea what an all-nighter even is. They started work the day they read about the assignment. The Perceptive person, however, may prefer to work at the last minute, and could actually come to life and be more creative and productive pulling an all-nighter.

Want to know how to spot a Judging vs. a Perceiving Type during communication?

Judging	**Perceiving**
Impatient with long procedures	Wants their own space for decisions
Hurried and wants a quick decision	Likes to explore more possibilities
Decides too quickly at times	Decides too much at the last minute at times
Likes closure	Likes processing

Test Yourself: Have you ever bought a key finder to help find your keys but then misplaced the key finder? Then you're probably a Perceptive person. Have you ever planned a vacation, including every detail of what you'll be doing, a year before you even depart? If so, you're probably a Judging person.

Again, Toni falls into both categories, and prefers a little bit of spontaneity and structure in different situations, whereas Diane is totally a Judging person. Once again, there's no right way to be in this category either; it's just important to know each preference, just like it is in the other three areas we've covered, so you can understand how different people operate. This area is particularly important when working in teams, so you know how other people are likely to go about projects.

We're proud to tell you that you've learned about all four areas, and by now should know your own MBTI combination, as well as practically being able to distinguish the combinations of the people around you. You should now be as positive and constructive as Tony Robbins while in the workplace. First, however, you should acknowledge which type you are, and understand your personal strengths in order to understand other people and how to best confront them and build effective cooperation and collaboration. Now that you've seen why it's important to have all types of people in a work environment, let's take a closer look at the different combinations.

TYPE

We know that you can be either an Introvert (I) or an Extrovert (E); a Sensor (S) or an Intuitive (N) (we have to use N here because I has already been used for Introvert); a Thinker (T) or a Feeler (F); and Judging (J) or Perceptive (P). Now, you need to take the letter representing the preference that you resemble most in each area, for example in Diane's case Extrovert, Sensor, Thinker, and Judging, and combine those letters to get your MBTI "type". So, Diane is an ESTJ, while Toni is an ENFP (with a couple of preference areas that are in between).

What the heck does that mean? How can you combine them all together like that? Well, that's the beauty of

Myers–Briggs. By figuring out which combination you are, you now know you have one of the 16 different types of brains set out below.

ISTJ	ISFJ	INFJ	INTJ
ISTP	ISFP	INFP	INTP
ESTP	ESFP	ENFP	ENTP
ESTJ	ESFJ	ENFJ	ENTJ

Figure out which one you are, and put an X in the box of the Type that best describes you. If you fall into one of the four types that are located in the corners of the grid, you may be a natural leader, because those types tend to do well as executives. It looks like one of Diane's type will be the next leader of the free world, since we're in the bottom left corner! If you fall into that group, you probably like to organize and get things done! If you fall into the upper left corner, you may be careful before risking too much change. If you fall into the upper right corner, you might be a great thinker about things, but may not actually get them done. And if you're in the bottom right corner, you like change, and don't mind doing something about it.

To learn the specific meaning behind each of the 16 types, check out http://www.myersbriggs.org/my-mbti-person-ality-type/mbti-basics/the-16-mbti-types.asp. This Myers–Briggs site gives an awesome description of what it means to belong to each type.

You might find it interesting to know what some famous personalities' types are.

ENTP:
Matthew Perry
Celine Dion
Tom Hanks
David Spade
John Candy

ENFJ:
Oprah
President Obama
Johnny Depp
Michael Jordan
Matthew McConaughey
Ben Affleck
Bob Saget

ENFP:
Robin Williams
Robert Downing Jr.
Sandra Bullock
Alicia Silverstone
Bill Cosby
Julie Andrews
Toni Rothpletz (had to throw us in the list; you'll find Diane below)

ENTJ:
Harrison Ford
Steve Martin
Jim Carrey
Sigourney Weaver
Steve Jobs
Jerry Seinfeld
Al Gore
Jay Leno
Rush Limbaugh

ESFJ:

Terry Bradshaw

Bill Clinton

Ronald Reagan

Sally Field

Carol Burnett

Mary Tyler Moore

ESTP:

Jack Nicholson

Eddie Murphy

Bruce Willis

Michael J. Fox

Madonna

Joan Rivers

John Madden

ESFP:

Goldie Hawn

Arsenio Hall

Woody Harrelson

Bob Hope

Adam Sandler

Meg Ryan

ESTJ:

Colin Powell

John D. Rockefeller

Lyndon B. Johnson

Carl Lewis

Diane Hamilton (here she is!)

ISTJ:

Evander Holyfield

George Washington

George H. W. Bush
(a lot of other U.S. Presidents)

ISTP:
Tom Cruise
Keith Richards
James Dean
Burt Reynolds
Clint Eastwood
Cher
Willie Nelson

INFJ:
Arnold Schwarzenegger
Lance Armstrong
Dan Aykroyd
Richard Gere
Woody Allen
Billy Crystal
Lady Gaga

INTP:
Tiger Woods
Albert Einstein
Theodore Kaczynski, the Unabomber!
Macauley Culkin
Sir Isaac Newton
Meryl Streep

INFP:
Julia Roberts
John F. Kennedy, Jr.
William Shakespeare
Neil Diamond
Tom Brokaw

INTJ:
Stewie Griffin (Had to throw Family Guy in there)
Alan Greenspan
Jodie Foster
Chevy Chase
Peter Jennings

ISFP:
Michael Jackson
Marilyn Monroe
Donald Trump
Ashton Kutcher
Britney Spears
John Travolta
Brooke Shields
Kevin Costner

ISFJ:
Barbara Bush
Princess Diana
Michael Jordan
O.J. Simpson

Just a quick note in relation to these lists. For the most part, these results are not self-disclosed. However, from what we've seen from published information about the people who are listed, they seem to be pretty accurate.

Hopefully, you've taken a MBTI or an MBTI-type test, and know your results. Now, not only do you know which famous people are like you, but you can now see how your type affects your work choices. Check out the following table to see some possible jobs you might like, and to find out how many people are out there in your category.

Type	Possible Job Interest	% of People
ISTJ	Bank Officer, Financial Manager	12–16%
ISFJ	Education, Health Care, Religion	10–13%
ESTP	Marketing, Business, Lawyer	5–7%
ESFP	Health Care, Teaching, Coaching	6–9%
INTJ	Scientific, Technical, Computers	3–4%
INFJ	Counseling, Teaching, Arts	2–3%
ENTP	Science, Management, Technology	4–7%
ENFP	Counseling, Teaching, Religion	6–8%
ISTP	Skilled Trades, Technical, Agriculture	5–7%
INTP	Science, Technology	5–6%
ESTJ	Management, Administration, Law	10–12%
ENTJ	Management, Leadership	3–5%
ISFP	Health Care, Business, Law	5–7%
INFP	Counseling, Writing, Arts	4–5%
ESFJ	Education, Health Care, Religion	10–12%
ENFJ	Religion, Arts	3–5%

Choosing the right job can be easier if you understand how the various parts that make up your type can affect your decisions. For example if you're an ST (Sensor, Thinker), you might look at businesses where you can use details. If you're an SF (Sensor, Feeler), you could do well in health care or education. NFs (Intuitive, Feeler) like to help people, while NTs (Intuitive, Thinker) like science, technology, and management.

Just for fun, if you're looking to stress out your fellow employees, here are the things that bug them.

Extroverts hate to work alone, and prefer not to communicate by email. They like to be interrupted occasionally, so as to have someone to talk to. They hate getting feedback in writing, and would rather get it personally.

Introverts prefer not to work with others. They don't like to talk on the phone a lot, or interact with others all that much. They don't want to act quickly without being able to think about it first, and prefer not to get verbal feedback.

Sensors don't like to do things in new ways. They hate not having detailed overviews, or having to figure out the meaning in the facts you give them. Label any chart you give them, or you'll drive them nuts! They don't like complex things.

Intuitives don't like always having to do things the proven way, and they hate details. Don't ask them to check on facts, because they don't like it. They prefer not to focus on the past, and aren't practical.

Thinkers don't like having to rely on personal experience to figure out situations, and don't like making adjustments based on individual needs. They aren't empathetic, and don't really care about personal values when making decisions.

Feelers don't like to analyze situations, and don't like worrying about standards or meeting criteria. They don't like to focus on flaws or be critiqued, and hate having to use only logic to make decisions.

Judging types can't handle flexibility, especially around timeframes or deadlines, and they don't like last-minute things. Don't even think about throwing a surprise party for this group of people!

Perceiving types hate to be organized or plan things. They don't like deadlines, and get pissed if you suggest they can't work well under last-minute timeframes. Don't ask them to plan ahead. I wouldn't ask this group to be in charge of the company Christmas party!

So, do the opposite of what's outlined above and you'll really stir up some office drama and maybe cause a few nervous breakdowns. Wouldn't that be fun? Yeah, in a world where you can purposely torture your colleagues at work and still keep a job. Seriously, why not take this information and use it to your advantage. If you know someone is a certain type, which isn't too hard to figure out now that you're a genius at understanding all the different types, why not just give them the information they want in the way that they want it? Wouldn't that make you the hero? Just think how people will appreciate you if you can tap into understanding them? By doing the opposite of what makes them crazy, you're doing the things that will help you get along with them in the end.

KEIRSEY TEMPERAMENT SORTER

There have been several different takes on how to utilize the information from tests like the MBTI. David Keirsey, a psychologist at California State, has created the Keirsey Temperament Sorter, which his site describes as "The most popular and useful personality assessment tool ever devised." It's been said that this test is similar to the Myers–Briggs assessment. Keirsey's 1978 book *Please Understand Me* popularized his work. A lot of his work had to do with conflict management, i.e. the ways in which people handle personal grievances. He is also a strong advocate for children, and not doping them with stimulants to help with their Attention Deficit Hyperactivity Disorder (ADHD).

Just as assessments like the Myers–Briggs indicator divide people into types, Keirsey's instrument does the same. He describes four temperaments, each of which includes subgroups. The four temperaments are: Artisans, with subgroups of Operators and Entertainers; Guardians, with subgroups of Administrators and Conservators; Idealists, with subgroups of Mentors and Advocates; and Rationals, with subgroups of Coordinators and Engineers.

Keirsey describes how people relate to one another, making the following claims about his temperament types based on how they tie into the Myers–Briggs types.

- **Initiators** (expressive and directive): Mobilizer (ENTJ), Supervisor (ESTJ), Promoter (ESTP), Educator (ENFJ)—Preemptive
- **Contenders** (attentive and directive): Planner (INTJ), Inspector (ISTJ), Crafter (ISTP), Adviser (INFJ)—Competitive

There are two Reactive Inquiring Roles:

- **Coworkers** (expressive and informative): Engineer (ENTP), Supplier (ESFJ), Performer (ESFP), Advocate (ENFP)—Collaborative
- **Responders** (attentive and informative): Designer (INTP), Protector (ISFJ), Composer (ISFP), Conciliator (INFP)—Accommodative

The biggest difference between Keirsey and Myers–Briggs was that Keirsey was more about observable behaviors than about information-processing preferences. If Jung's model was more concerned with the differences between Introverts and Extroverts, Keirsey's focus was more about the differences between Intuitive and Sensing types. Keirsey was also more about temperament than attitude. To find out more about Keirsey's 70-question test, you can check out www.keirsey.com.

"Personality tests typically only distinguish four categories of temperament but do not distinguish which melancholy person is actually high in ambition. For example, business people know that they want an extrovert to fill the sales position, but they cannot tell from a temperament test which ones will be persistent from those who will be insistent." (Hodu.com, 2010) Utilizing assessments that analyze personality preferences may be helpful, but it may also be important to understand the impact of emotional intelligence in the workplace. According to EQI.org, "Unmet emotional needs cause the majority of problems at work."

CHAPTER 3:
EMOTIONAL INTELLIGENCE

"Surround yourself with amazing intelligent men and women. The people I work with not only are smarter than I am, possessing both intellectual and emotional intelligence, but also share my determination to succeed. I will not make an important decision without them."

— George Steinbrenner

You've probably heard the term Emotional Intelligence (EI) used a lot lately. If not, well now you have, and soon you'll be an Emotional Intelligence expert! Having a high Emotional Quotient, or EQ, has become as important as having a high IQ in the working world. IQ stands for Intelligence Quotient, but you probably knew that, because you have a high IQ, right? Anyway, having a high EQ is seen as probably more important than IQ in determining your success at work these days.

Before you can understand what Emotional Intelligence (EI) is, first you must understand intelligence in general. Intelligence has often been defined as the ability to learn or understand something. Sometimes, it involves reasoning, or the ability to perform certain acts. Others have described it as the ability to solve problems. Not everyone believes there is just one form of intelligence, indeed there are those who believe in multiple intelligences.

Most and Zeidner (1995) distinguished between intelligence and personality. Many other researchers have attempted to discover how certain traits differ based on how we react from an intelligence standpoint and a personality standpoint. To better understand intelligence, cognitive and mental-ability tests have been created while personality tests have been created to better understand personality. There have been a lot of critics of personality assessments, because they can be vague or subjective. Studying people's emotions can be one of the most difficult things of all.

When looking at intelligence tests, the types of intelligence you've probably heard most about include IQ (intelligence quotient) and EQ (emotional quotient). To better understand both IQ and EQ, it's important to look at the importance that has historically been placed on both these areas. IQ testing became popular in the early 1900s in France. It has been claimed that these tests were originally designed to identify those "special" students that weren't so bright so they could be placed in special classes away from the more intellectually gifted "normal" students. In those days, they thought that IQ couldn't be improved, and was based on the misfortune of having stupid parents, a terrible mistake that crazy guys like Hitler subsequently embraced. Thankfully, we've grown to realize that this isn't true.

What was complicated about these tests, though, was that in order to measure someone's intelligence, first they had to decide on a definition of intelligence. What does the IQ test measure? Well, much of what it's intended to show us is how well a person has been able to learn something, and what their potential is for learning. The good news is, our IQs seem to be going up. Yay! The bad news is, they aren't sure if those results are just a mistake based on inaccurate testing. Bummer!

Although the study of EQ can be traced back to the early 1900s, the real popularity of emotional intelligence has only developed over the last couple of decades. Peter Salovey and John Mayer actually coined the term emotional intelligence in 1990, however, Daniel Goleman was one of the first people to bring this term into the mainstream. There have been many variations of what is classified as emotional intelligence, such as social intelligence or having multiple intelligences, a term coined by a guy named Howard Gardner on the basis of his work in the 1980s.

What can be confusing about emotional intelligence is that no one seems to agree on what the heck it is. Of course, that seems to be a common problem. Wouldn't it be nice if there was always just one definition of something? Well, good luck with that, because there are several definitions of emotional intelligence. Here, we will look at the top three models of emotional intelligence as proposed by Goleman, Mayer & Salovey, and Bar-On. For example, according to Salovey et al. (2007), Goleman states that "These abilities are called emotional intelligence, which includes self-control, zeal, persistence, and the ability to motivate oneself." Mayer & Salovey define emotional intelligence as "the set of abilities that account for how people's emotional perception and understanding vary in their accuracy." More formally, they define emotional intelligence as "the ability to perceive and express emotion, assimilate emotion in thought, understand and reason with emotion, and regulate emotion in the self and others." Bar-On (yes, that really is his name) defines emotional intelligence as "an array of noncognitive capabilities, competencies, and skills that influence one's ability to succeed in coping with environmental demands and pressures." If you're now scratching your head and thinking "huh?", for ease of explanation, we'll go with the following definition: **having the ability to**

understand the emotions within you as well as the ability to understand emotions within others. Whew, that's much easier!

Why can't everyone just agree on one definition? Probably because there's so much involved in understanding emotions. There is the ability to perceive, understand, and manage your emotions, but there are also self-management and self- or social-awareness issues. How one handles conflict and stress is also mixed into the pot. It's no wonder that researchers keep redefining emotional intelligence, because no one really knows what to include and what to exclude.

To break things down even more, we're now going to look at the components that each of these authorities includes in their definition of EI.

Goleman's Definition

Daniel Goleman's definition of emotional intelligence includes the following elements:

Knowing One's Emotions – Do you recognize your feelings as you are feeling them? Are you able to stay in the moment and monitor these feelings?

Managing Emotions – Can you appropriately handle your feelings and soothe yourself should they upset you? Can you shake off negativity or anxiety, or does it linger with you?

Motivating Oneself – How strong are your impulses? Can you delay gratification and be able to go with the flow in order to attain a goal?

Recognizing Emotions in Others – Are you empathetic and tuned in to what others are feeling?

Handling Relationships – Can you manage emotions in others and still interact well with them?

Mayer & Salovey's Definition

John Mayer and Peter Salovey's definition of emotional intelligence includes the following elements:

Perception and Expression of Emotion – How well do you express what you are feeling? Do you keep your thoughts and feelings bottled up? Can you identify not only your own emotions but those in others?

Assimilating Emotion in Thought – How well do you prioritize your emotions into productive things? Are you using your emotions as a way to judge things?

Understanding and Analyzing Emotions – Can you label your emotions to better understand them? Sometimes emotions have feelings that go along with them. Can you handle them?

Reflecting Regulation of Emotions – Are you open to feeling emotions? Or do you prefer to be an emotionless robot? Can you grow through monitoring the things you feel?

Bar-On's Definition

Reuven Bar-On's definition of emotional intelligence includes the following elements:

Intrapersonal Skills – What are intrapersonal skills? Things that Bar-On includes in this group would be emotional self-awareness, assertiveness, self-regard, self-actualization and independence. Are you aware of the emotions that you are feeling? Do you bottle them inside? How do you see yourself? Are you self-confident and independent, or do you hold yourself back? Basically, having intrapersonal skills is having the ability to understand how your emotions are affecting you.

Interpersonal Skills – What are interpersonal skills? Bar-On includes things such as interpersonal relationships, social responsibility and empathy. How do you get along with other people? Do you care about their feelings? Can you put yourself into their situation and see things from their perspective?

Ability to Handle Stress – What does it mean to have the ability to handle stress? This includes the areas of stress tolerance and impulse control. Do you freak out every time someone asks you to do something you don't want to do? Are you able to keep your temper under control?

Adaptability – If you score high on adaptability scales it means you're good at problem solving and reality testing, and have flexibility. These skills would be important if you're going through any kind of major change at work. During times like these, who isn't?!

Maintaining General Mood – General mood includes having general happiness and optimism. Do you come into work on Monday dreading the week ahead? Do you have a glass-half-empty kind of attitude? Do people ever refer to you as Debbie Downer?

Basically, the test that Bar-On created measures whether someone has high skills in each of these areas. Diane used Bar-On's Eq-i model in her research for her dissertation regarding sales people, because it made sense that having the ability to understand your own emotions as well as those in others would be a good thing in such an interpersonal thing as sales. And, surprise, surprise, the results did show that having a higher EQ made for more successful sales people. Further, not only did having high interpersonal skills make a significant difference, but so did having a good general mood. Duh ... let's think about that for a moment. If I'm in a good mood, I come across better when I'm trying to sell something to someone. Yep, that makes sense. If you aren't a very upbeat person, you might not want to go into sales.

What does this all mean?

Why would anyone want to even worry about emotional intelligence? Either you have it or you don't, right? Wrong. Everyone has some level of emotional intelligence. It's just that some of us have more than others. Think about that guy next to you at work; yep, not a lot of EI going on there. We've all met someone at work who has no interpersonal communication skills whatsoever. They might come across as self-absorbed and narcissistic, and are likely the ones who've forced us to live with the nauseating expression 'There is no "I" in "team."' If they had any idea of how ego-centric they were, that expression would probably never have come about.

Is there any help for them? The good news is, yes, EQ can be developed! Researchers such as Marcia Hughes and Daniel Goleman have written books about developing workers' EQ. So, why would you want to increase your EQ?

Well, for one thing, employers sometimes care more about your EQ than your IQ. That's not to say they want to hire morons who all get along well together. Rather, they're now realizing that having some of these interpersonal skills can be as important as having a good brain in their head. In fact, some employers are now giving EQ tests to their prospective employees, so those of you who have little to no EI, pay attention. You can fix that!

One thing you can do is to try and put yourself in someone else's position in your mind. How are your actions affecting that person? Do you care? If not, you should. If you don't, it's going to come back to bite you later. Try to think of what is important to that person. Some of this ties in with understanding personality preferences, which are discussed in the Myers–Briggs chapter of this book. If a person is a "feeling" person, they may be basing their decisions on their own values. By understanding that, you're developing your ability to put yourself into their shoes, and becoming more emotionally intelligent. Good job!

Having empathy for others is a big part of being emotionally intelligent. Having empathy means you have compassion for others, and are able to see things from their perspective. Not everybody is going to have the same types of feelings or responses to things. If you look at someone's reaction and find it to be silly because it is different from your own, that is not an emotionally intelligent response. You must show respect for others' feelings in order to become more emotionally intelligent.

It's also important to understand what you are feeling, and to acknowledge good and bad feelings. Remember, our definition of emotional intelligence includes understanding your own emotions. By facing what you are feeling and realizing that it's okay to feel both the good and the bad emotions, you're developing your own EQ. It's okay to stop bottling up your emotions! Do we sound like therapists?

Are you looking for non-verbal clues when communicating? How many of us have seen the guy who blabs on and on while the person he is blabbing to looks like they want to slit their wrists? Part of the problem here is that the guy who's doing the talking isn't looking for non-verbal clues. Always remember that some people are actually polite, and may not tell you what a pain you really are. Next time you're doing all of the talking, look at them and take note. Are their arms crossed? Are they looking at their watch or not making eye contact? Are they trying to file, or type, or just do their job, and you're interrupting them? Are they just nodding their head, and not asking you questions in response to what you're saying? These are all non-verbal clues that indicate that you're annoying them, or keeping them from doing something that they either need to or would rather be doing.

Speaking of blabbing ... do you just talk, talk, talk without listening? Are you more concerned about getting your point across than hearing what someone else has to say? Seriously, do you really think that what you have to say is so important? Try listening to someone else for a change. I thought we talked about this to all you Extroverts already? You might be surprised at how smart people actually are if you would just let them speak.

Handling stress is another important part of emotional intelligence. How do you cope with stressful situations? Does your boss telling you that you have to work an extra hour cause you to hyperventilate? If so, stop, breathe, and think about it. Do you like making money? Well then, work an extra hour and get over it. Is it really worth freaking out over? Think about people in other countries who work 12-hour days for $1. You could be that guy. Put yourself in someone else's shoes, someone who has it worse than you do. Sometimes that helps to put things into perspective. Many times, our stress is an over-reaction. At work, there are bound to be stressful situations, many of them revolving around change. The best way to handle change is to understand why something is happening.

Communication is the key. If you don't understand why something is happening ... ask. The more information you have, the less stressed you'll be.

Look at why you're feeling the way you are, instead of why someone else is making you feel a certain way. Have you ever heard someone at work say, "I can't believe he/she did that to me?" Step back and think about what was done. Was it really done to you? Are they really the one making you upset, or is it your reaction to what they did that's making you upset. You can't control what other people do, but you can control your reaction to what they do. Always keep communication lines open. By getting mad and shutting down, you're spoiling your chance of working well with others. Having low interpersonal skills will only hurt you in the end. Do you really think the boss wants to promote the guy or gal who is pouting in the corner because someone hurt their feelings? Don't be a baby. Things can't always be just the way you want them, and sometimes you are going to encounter situations you don't necessarily respond well to. Just take a minute to control your reaction, and deal with it.

Remember, it's up to you to create your own happiness. The mistake many people make is expecting others to make them happy. You may be thinking that if only you could get promoted, you'd be happy, or if you didn't have to work 8-hour days, your life could be wonderful. Perhaps both of these are likely true to some extent, however they're probably not realistic. It's up you to see the glass half-full, rather than half-empty. By being optimistic and happy, you're more likely to get promoted and maybe once you're the boss, your job will be so wonderful you'll want to work 9-hour days.

It's important to maintain a high level of self-awareness. Do you meditate, or keep a journal of troubling emotions? Meditation can help you stop and really think about the things that are troubling you. If you keep a journal, notice whether you are writing positive or negative things. If they're negative, you need to focus on why that's so. Are you looking at the bad side of things? This can become a habit. Think about those friends of yours who always post negative status updates on Facebook. Things like "I hate Mondays" or "Thank God it's Friday" are indicators of someone who is looking at things in a negative way. Imagine if they have that attitude at work. If they do, they probably don't even realize it, but I guarantee you that those around them will notice. Negativity comes through loud and clear! And no one likes to be around a downbeat person.

Just because you feel negative emotions, that doesn't make you a bad person. Everyone has negative feelings at times. The key is how you deal with them. Do you wear them on your sleeve, with a "poor me" attitude, or do you realize that in order to appreciate the good in life, sometimes we have to experience the bad?

If you experience a negative emotion, take a moment to think about it. Try to distance yourself from it. Look at it as if it were your friend's problem. What would you advise them to do? Many of us are able to tell others how to deal with things, but we have a harder time telling ourselves.

An important part of improving your EQ is to work on your people and social skills. Don't rush to judgment. Are you over-reacting to something that someone has said? Many times, people simply say stupid things because they don't take the time to think before they speak. If you read the earlier chapter on Myers–Briggs, you probably know that Extroverts are infamous for such behavior. Does that mean they're bad people? No, they just spoke as they thought, instead of thinking and then speaking. Now it's your turn practice thinking before you speak or react.

Perhaps the person who said something stupid was an attention seeker. Ah, another indicator of low EQ! If you're an attention seeker, maybe you need to get your recognition through a job such as sales. You could also write a book ... as you can see, we're still working on our issues.

Try to remember that, although you want attention, other people may not care. People like to hear about themselves, and not about you! Next time you rush to tell someone at work about your weekend of adventures, stop and ask them a question instead. How was their weekend? How are their kids? Remember, it's not all about you!

Is learning all this new stuff stressing you out? If so, how you react to stress is another indicator of your EQ. You're probably familiar with the old phrase, "Don't sweat the small stuff." Well, it's true. If you're freaking out about little things you can't control, you need to step back and rethink it. Do you really have control over that situation? If not, why are you trying to control it? There are healthy ways to deal with stress, rather than being a control freak!

The important thing to remember is to take responsibility for the things you do, and for how those things affect others around you. If you realize that you need to work on a lot of these things, don't freak out. Take them one at a time. Eventually, you will have increased not only your EQ, but also your appeal to those who are considering hiring you!

There's no denying that emotional intelligence is critical to success. Hodu.com (2010) recently summarized several studies where having a high EQ was confirmed as being important. Employers who hire employees with strong emotional intelligence skills just might improve their bottom line. One of the more recent examples they mentioned was "A Texas-based Fortune 500 Company that had utilized personality assessments for candidate selection for years with little results in reducing the high turnover in their sales force. After turning to an emotional intelligence-based selection assessment and an EQ training and development program, they increased retention by 67 percent in the first year, which they calculated added $32 million to their bottom line in reduced turnover costs and increased sales revenues" (Hodo.com, 2010).

Why should you care about studies like these? Because companies care about their bottom line. Companies just might be looking at your EQ to see if you're going to be an asset to them. That means you need to be working on developing it. We suggest doing some of the things we mentioned earlier to help increase your score.

CHAPTER 4:
THE BIG FIVE FACTORS

*"It is better to be hated for who you are,
than to be loved for someone you are not."*

— Anonymous

In the 1970s, two separate research teams came up with what we now call The Big Five Factors of Personality. Actually, some of the research on this began as early as 1936. You may have heard the terms "Big Five" or "Five-Factor Model." These are basically the same thing. This is probably one of the best-known theories in this field. Next time you're at one of your work happy hours and someone throws one of those terms at you, you'll be cool, because you'll know what he or she is talking about. This model or theory is one of the most researched and widely acknowledged models describing personality. Thousands of people have been studied to provide the data that led to the Big Five. The model identifies traits of human personality in a score referred to as the Big Five Inventory (BFI). So, if you hear the term "BFI", it has nothing to do with Best Friends Indefinitely, or anything else you can come up with. With this test, people are scored on 44 items, which reveals their BFI. The model is based upon our personality having five traits:

- **Openness to Experience**
- **Conscientiousness**

- **Extraversion**
- **Agreeableness**
- **Neuroticism**

Let's jump into the qualities that accompany each trait, and what it means to score high or low in each area. Openness to Experience, which we will call "O", includes things like how we appreciate art, our emotions, ideas, and curiosities. It has a lot to do with how imaginative one is, and how intellectually curious they are. Low scores in this area may mean the person is more traditional, with not a lot of interest in the arts. They may also resist change more than someone with a higher level. High scores tend to be recorded when a person has a stronger imagination, a rich vocabulary, and is idea driven.

In the work environment, a person who has high levels of "O", as we will call it, may tend to be very imaginative, and yet may also spend a lot of time daydreaming. This person may be the one looking out the window thinking about things they would rather be doing than working. They are intellectually curious, and idealists. The good news is that they like variety, and will try new things, so don't just think of this group as airheads. If you have a work project you don't want to do, and are looking to delegate, this person may be your go-to guy. They're up for a challenge!

If you have to work with someone with a low "O" level, you may find that they're not really into a challenge. They may come across as more conservative, with a narrow focus. Don't be showing this guy your doodling artwork from the last meeting you attended, because he probably won't appreciate it. His main focus is the present, and there's not a lot of foresight going on with him.

Conscientiousness, or "C", is seen in a person who displays self-discipline and is achievement-oriented. Those people with low scores in this area may not be well prepared, or able to get things done in a timely manner. They may be seen as messy or disorganized. Those with high scores in this area may be detail-oriented, smart, and reliable. They may take this too far though, and come across as perfectionists, or even workaholics.

The high "C" colleague comes across as very capable, well-organized, and driven. Her desk is immaculate. Don't try moving her stapler; you might send her into a complete panic. The good news is, she's your go-to gal for planning things, because she's always reliable. She will not only do what you ask her to do, but she'll complete it on time. Keep in mind though, there are the few that have an untidy desk, or come off as a mess, but when you ask them to find a document or something in a hurry, they know exactly where it is. Some people prefer certain systems that only make sense to them, and although they might have what looks like a chaotic mess of a desk, they're completely organized, and know where everything is in their head.

The low "C" colleague is a different story. This gal's desk is a mess too, and she doesn't know where to find anything. If you ask her to find you the most recent copy of something, it may take her a while to shuffle through her unorganized clutter. Don't expect her to be on-time to meetings, either. There's not a lot of self-discipline with this chick. Can you say procrastinator? She can! She's spontaneous to a fault. There's no deliberation in anything she does. Low "C's" love doing spur-of-the-moment things, and live an unstructured life.

Extraversion, or "E", is a term that has been used in many different models, including Myers–Briggs ... remember? We'll do a quick recap here, because the Big Five Model has similar definitions to Myers–Briggs studies in terms of what it means to be Extraverted. In the Big Five Model, Extraversion is about wanting to be around other people, being full of energy, being talkative, and drawing attention to themselves. The opposite of Extraversion would be ... Introversion. Duh! This person may not be seen as the life of the party, or looking for attention, but you already knew that, because you made it through the Myers–Briggs chapter. So, we'll skip straight to what it means to possess the trait of Agreeableness.

Agreeableness, or "A", is a term that encompasses how cooperative one may be. Does the person get along well with others, or do they try to antagonize them? This part of one's personality is also discussed in the chapter about Concern for Impact. Being Agreeable means caring about other people's feelings, and how your personality impacts others. Those with a low "A" level are not really concerned with other's emotions or well-being, and tend to insult people without really caring about it. They can become very isolated, as others may learn to avoid them.

Those with a high "A" level are your honest, helpful, nice guys. They usually have the best of intentions, and are a pleasure to be around. They will also tell you like it is, in a friendly way. This is the self-effacing guy; truly humble. The best part about this guy is that he's willing to help others. If you need to delegate, this guy would love to help you out. They also may come across as very sensitive, so bring some tissues for this guy, just in case ... only kidding!

Those with a low "A" level are your cynics. They come across as stretching the truth. Next time you're on YouTube, look up Jon Lovitz talking about his girlfriend being Morgan Fairchild.

For those of you too young to remember, Jon Lovitz is from *Saturday Night Live*, and Morgan Fairchild was a good-looking actress. This guy was definitely stretching the truth!

The low "A" guy does not want to get involved. There's no competitive spirit there, so he's not going to be looking to win any contests. Hopefully he's not in sales! There's not a lot of modesty on his part either, and he can come across as insensitive. He'd be ripping that tissue right out of the high "A" guy's hand and telling him to get over it.

Neuroticism, or "N", has a lot to do with negative emotions such as anxiety, depression, and anger. Someone with a low "N" level may have difficulty controlling their emotions, and may often seem moody, or irritable, or stressed out. Someone with a higher "N" level may appear to be more calm and collected, more in control of their emotional state.

If your fellow employee has a high "N" level, this individual is probably a worrier, angers easily, and has difficulty with coping. Ahh, isn't that the ideal person you want sitting next to you at work? A person with a high "N" level is easily discouraged as well. If you do have to work with this individual, they might be an easily defeated competitor, because they would let their worrying get the best of them. Interestingly, there was a study published in 2007 in ScienceDirect about the impact of the Big Five in terms of predicting who would blog. "The results of two studies indicate that people who are high in openness to new experience and high in neuroticism are likely to be bloggers. Additionally, the neuroticism relationship was moderated by gender, indicating that women who are high in neuroticism are more likely to be bloggers as compared to those low in neuroticism, whereas there was no difference for men" (Guadagno et al., 2007).

If your fellow employee has a low "N" level, this person is much calmer, and you won't be able to piss them off so easily. They may also come across as guilt-free, and not easily embarrassed. They're the ones you want to assign to emergency fireman duty for the office, because they work well under stress, and don't freak out in a crisis. Think ER doctor here; they remain calm under intense pressure.

Is everyone at a high or low level in terms of these measures? No, most people are actually somewhere in the middle, and may score higher or lower in different situations. If you're midrange on "N", you may find that stress only gets to you on occasion. Midrange "E" people may occasionally like to be alone, while midrange "O" people could be innovative at times, but not always. A midrange "A" could be willing to concede ground in a situation where all parties would benefit, while a midrange "C" person might be able to find work/life balance.

Employers can learn a lot from the Big Five Model, because studies have shown that having higher levels in certain areas can correlate with superior job performance. Extroversion has been shown to predict success in sales-oriented positions, while this trait, as well as Openness to Experience, has also been used to predict training proficiency.

When considering whether some of our personality traits are a result of nature or nurture, it has been found that these five traits are pretty close to being half and half. This means that although you may have a chance of inheriting certain personality traits, you can also develop these traits over time. Men and women also show differences in their levels in some of these areas. Women tend to be more Neurotic and Agreeable, while men tend to be more Extraverted and Conscientious. A researcher named Frank Sulloway looked at birth order, and suggested that firstborns tend to be more Conscientious, but less open to new ideas, although his studies were later called into question due to the subjectivity of the rating of personality traits by fellow family members in his experiments. Other major studies have since found no correlation between birth order and these factors.

One of the big issues in relation to the Big Five Model has to do with teams. Like Myers–Briggs and other such assessments, it can provide a way to understand and make the most of our differences. Most teams are made up of very diverse people, which can mean a lot of different backgrounds, skills, and personalities. By taking these tests, team members can not only better understand themselves, but can also better understand others in the group. If everyone on the team had the same personality, it might not be the best group, in terms of effectiveness. If everyone had a high "E" level, you could be sure that a whole lot of talking and interrupting would be going on in this group, while if everyone had a low "A" level, no one would want to step up and take the lead. By mixing up the personalities on a team, you're actually making the team more operationally effective.

Can this model categorize all parts of one personality? "Most, if not all, of the personality traits that you would use to describe someone else could be reliably categorized into one of the FFM personality dimensions" (Hughes, Ginnett, and Curphy, 2009, p. 208). In case you didn't catch on to that acronym, FFM = Five Factor Model. Does that mean that one model can explain how our personality works? That's been the criticism of this theory. Many have complained that there are more parts to a personality than this model contains. What about Honesty, Religiosity, Sense of Humor, and Motivation? These are all things that may not be factored into this model.

What about the dark side of one's personality? Many personality assessments don't look at the negatives as much as preferences and aptitudes. However, according to Hogan Assessment Systems, the following comprise what they call "Dark-Side Personality Traits:"

- Excitable – has mood swings
- Skeptical – doesn't trust others
- Cautious – fears making dumb mistakes
- Reserved – too objective – may hurt others' feelings
- Leisurely – overly agreeable but shows no initiative
- Bold – takes on too much
- Mischievous – pushes limits and breaks rules
- Colorful – unhealthy need to be center of attention
- Imaginative – too off-beat or eccentric
- Diligent – need to be too precise
- Dutiful – reluctant to rock the boat.

When looking at effective leaders in the business world, one would not want to see too many of the above personality traits. "Dark-side personality traits are irritating, counterproductive behavioral tendencies that interfere with a leader's ability" (Hughes, Ginnett and Curphy, 2009, p. 218). Therefore, if as a young adult your goal is to enter a position of leadership, you may want to assess yourself to ensure you don't have a lot of the above-mentioned traits.

Although there is no universal personality profiling that everyone agrees covers everything, the FFM has a pretty broad acceptance. "Another advantage of the Five Factor Model is that it appears universally applicable across cultures. People from Asian, Western European, Middle Eastern, Eastern European, or South American cultures seem to use the same five personality dimensions to categorize, profile or describe others" (Hughes, Ginnett, and Curphy, 2009, p. 216). If you're interested in finding out more about the Big Five Model, there are some free tests with feedback at www.signalpatterns.com. For those looking to learn more about utilizing the Big Five Model at work, check out *The Owner's Manual for Personality at Work* by Pierce J. Howard and Jane Mitchell Howard.

CHAPTER 5:
BIRTH ORDER

"Your birth is a mistake you'll spend your whole life trying to correct."

— Chuck Palahnuik

Can your birth order have anything to do with your success in life? That's a question many researchers have asked, but is it a valid question, or just a pop culture phenomenon? Many of these theories began with Freud and Jung, who both suggested that birth order may have something to do with personality, and these theories have created quite a bit of controversy in the field of psychology over the years. As mentioned in the previous chapter, a researcher named Frank Sulloway suggested that there was an influence based on birth order, however his research was later seen as inconclusive, due to the input received from fellow family members, who may have made subjective judgments. Another researcher, Judith Rich Harris, felt that although birth order may have some affect on personality, the results don't necessarily last into adulthood.

Everything from intelligence to sexuality has been studied based on birth order. As recently as 2007, studies showed that the oldest child had a higher IQ than their younger siblings, but as far as sexuality is concerned, there haven't been any really accepted studies that have shown a correlation. A book by

Edward M. Miller has suggested that later-born sons may be more likely to be homosexual, but the jury is still out on this one, and more research needs to be done. For now, we will focus on how birth order affects our personality and careers.

There have been some studies on how birth order affects one's career. Careerbuilder has found that first-borns are more likely to make a salary of over $100,000 a year. They also found that while middle children don't make as much, they tend to be more satisfied with their income, while the youngest seem to enjoy outdoor-based or artistic positions.

Interestingly, the birth order of serial killers has been studied. The statistics for this group are:

>   First-born 32%
>   Middle-born 28%
>   Last-born or Youngest 25%
>   Only Child 15%

Famous first-borns include:

>   Nick Lachey
>   Jessica Simpson
>   Josh Hartnett
>   Brandy
>   Oprah
>   Sylvester Stallone
>   Bruce Willis
>   Bill Cosby

Here are some famous middle-born children:

>   Brittany Spears
>   Elijah Wood

David Letterman
Madonna
Princess Diana
Bill Gates
Jay Leno

Here's an interesting side note; 50% of all US Presidents were middle-born children.

Famous last-born children include:

Halle Berry
Cameron Diaz
Mark McGrath of Sugar Ray
Jim Carrey
Drew Carey
Rosie O'Donnell
Whoopi Goldberg
Eddie Murphy
Billy Crystal

Here are some famous only children:

Robin Williams
Brooke Shields
Freddie Prinze, Jr.
Alicia Keys
Tiger Woods
Leonardo Da Vinci
Charlize Theron
Natalie Portman
Sarah Michelle Gellar
Robert De Niro

Perhaps you're a first-born, or you may have to deal with a first-born at work. It should be noted that some criteria have been established that determine what is considered first-born. These include being the oldest of your gender in the family, or being five or more years younger than your nearest older sibling. If this sounds confusing, take the following example. One may have older brothers but is the oldest female in her family; while you might consider her the youngest, she's considered to be the first-born female. For another example, take Diane, who is considered a first-born, even though she's the youngest of three, because her next oldest sibling is five years older than her. If you're five or more years younger than your nearest older sibling, many consider you to be a first-born. According to Dr. Kevin Leman, who wrote *The Birth Order Book*, the qualities of a first-born include "being a perfectionist, reliable, conscientious, list-maker, well organized, hard driving, a natural leader, critical, serious, scholarly, logical, doesn't like surprises, a techie." It appears that Dr. Leman has been following Diane around, because that list couldn't be more accurate!

First-borns have been considered aggressive go-getters, which can lead to a high-stress lifestyle. They probably caused a lot of stress when they were young as well, because first-time parents usually don't really know what they're doing. Parents learn how to be parents through having their first child, and so first-borns may receive a lot more attention because of this.

Kevin Leman (2009) outlined the positives and negatives of first-borns:

Positives: They are natural leaders and often high achievers. The majority of politicians, spokespersons and managing directors are first-borns. They frequently live with a sense of entitlement and even superiority. They often come in two flavors: compliant nurturers/caregivers or aggressive movers and shakers. Both are in control; they just use different methods. As a rule, first-borns are picky, precise people – they pay attention to detail – tend to be punctual, organized, and competent. They want to see things done right the first time. They don't like surprises.

Negatives: They are often moody and occasionally lack sensitivity. They can be intimidating, particularly by pushing people too hard or refusing to take no for an answer. Sometimes they can be a bit 'know-it-all', and often they are poor at delegating – largely because they don't trust other people as much as they trust themselves. They also tend to be bossy, perfectionists and overly-conscientious.

It has often been said that the middle-born child gets ignored. Some suggest that the first-born gets a lot of attention due to the 'newness' of having a baby, and then if there are three children, the last-born or "baby" takes up the rest of the parents' attentions. Dr. Leman claims that the middle child's qualities include "mediator, compromising, diplomatic, avoids conflict, independent, loyal to peers, many friends, a maverick, secretive, unspoiled." Because of their position in the sibling line, they tend to be more independent, and can be helpful in mediating between the other two siblings. The good news is that they tend to have fewer issues and hang-ups than their elder sibling.

Here are Dr. Leman's positives and negatives about middle-borns:

Positives: The classic middle-born is very relational, tends to be a people-pleaser and usually hates confrontation.

Their basic need is to keep life smooth and their motto might be 'peace at any price'. They are usually very calm, will roll with the punches and are amiable, down-to-earth and great listeners. They are skilled at seeing both sides of a problem and eager to make everybody happy. That makes them good mediators and negotiators.

Negatives: They tend to be less driven than first-borns, but are much more eager to be liked – or at least have people be happy with them. They have a difficult time setting boundaries. They can drift into becoming 'co-dependent' as they try to please everybody. They are not good at making decisions that will offend others. They also tend to blame themselves when others fail.

The last-born child or "baby" seems to get all of the attention. Dr. Leman states that the qualities of a last-born include "being manipulative, charming, blames others, attention seeker, tenacious, people person, natural salesperson, precocious, engaging, affectionate, loves surprises." Toni is the last-born or the "baby" of the family, and this describes her very well. She's very affectionate, a total people person, and does very well in sales positions.

One of the reasons why last-borns are different is that parents have loosened up, and tend to be less nervous around their youngest child. With the first-born, everything is sterilized and baby-proofed, but by the time they have their last child, the parents finally stop carrying that bottle of sanitizer with them everywhere they go; that pacifier that falls on the floor is suddenly just fine for the baby after a quick wipe on a sleeve. The five-second rule they might have used with the middle-born is now replaced with the concept that a little dirt can't hurt ya with the last-born. The parents may be thinking, 'Heck, it might even build up their immune system.'

Parents may also be realizing that this is the last child they'll be having, and they may be giving them more attention due to the fact that they know they won't be seeing all these cute things again somewhere down the road. Since a major trait of these last-borns is persistence, parents may be encouraging this by giving them so much attention.

Dr. Leman outlines the following positives and negatives of last-borns:

Positives: Last-borns are the world's cheerleaders. They have strong people skills and love to entertain and talk to others. They make friends easily and immediately make others feel at home. They're an extrovert, energized by the presence of other people and they're probably not afraid to take risks.

Negatives: Last-borns tend to get bored quickly. They have a strong fear of rejection and a short attention span. When the fun stops, they've had enough and want to check out. To some extent they're self-centered. They may harbor unrealistic expectations of finding a relationship that is always fun – and of course, such relationships simply do not last.

Again, this describes Toni down to a "T".

Lastly, the only-borns also have their own unique qualities. Dr. Leman describes them as "little adult by age seven, very thorough, deliberate, high achiever, self-motivated, fearful, cautious, voracious reader, black-and-white thinker, talks in extremes, can't bear to fail, has very high expectations for self, more comfortable with people who are older or younger." At times, these only-children are perceived in a negative way, and some people may think they have missed out on experiences that only come with having siblings. I guarantee, however, that there are some experiences we've all had with our siblings that we're willing to give up!

Dr. Leman (2009) outlines the following positives and negatives for only-borns:

Positives: Only-borns are the mega-movers of the world. They are task-orientated; tend to be extremely well organized, highly conscientious and dependable. They are keen on facts, ideas and details and feel extremely comfortable with responsibility.

Negatives: The negative characteristics of only-borns can be tough to handle. They are often unforgiving, very demanding, hate to admit they're wrong and usually don't accept criticism well. To others, they seem very sensitive and indeed, their feelings are easily hurt."

Now that we know the different characteristics of each birth-order, it should shed more light on why people act a certain way. It may also have helped you recognize some of the qualities listed for your birth-order and hopefully you've gained further insight into your personality traits and attributes. You may not know what your coworkers' birth-orders are, and you might not be comfortable asking them either, but now you know that birth-order plays a part in making up our personalities, it might be a fun new little game for you at work to try guessing what birth-order each colleague is, based on your daily interactions with them and observing the traits that most clearly define them.

CHAPTER 6:
PERSONALITY POWER AND GOALS

"A substantial proportion of people do what they are told to do, irrespective of the content of the act and without limitations of conscience, so long as they perceive that the command comes from a legitimate authority."

— Stanley Milgram

Part of understanding our personality is understanding power. Who has it? How do they get and keep it? If we're going to be explaining how power affects personality, we would be remiss if we did not cover the Milgram Experiment. We talked briefly about the Milgram Experiment earlier in the book, but now we'll elaborate.

In the early 60s, a guy named Stanley Milgram did some research into the willingness of people to follow directions given by those in authority. If you were asked to shock someone with 400 volts of electricity, would you do it just because someone in a white lab coat told you to do it as part of an experiment? What he was looking for was how authority leads to obedience. Isn't that kind of what happens to you at work? You're at the mercy of your leader or manager. You do what they tell you to do, because they are your superior, and you figure you should listen. Part of what makes up your personality is the part that is willing to obey commands that may not necessarily make sense to you.

First off, how cool is it that they thought they got to shock people? I'm sure you can think of a few people you'd like to shock some sense into ... if it didn't hurt them too badly, right? But shocking an absolute stranger? That doesn't seem very humane. We'd like to think we'd be the test subjects that wouldn't have pushed the button to deliver the shock to the recipients. The thing was, though, although the people thought they were delivering a shock, they weren't delivering any voltage at all. The people who were supposedly being shocked were actors who were just pretending to be shocked. The people Dr. Milgram used as the "shockers" in his experiments were only paid $4.50, and were found through advertisements placed in newspapers. So, let's stop right there. What quality of person are you going to get from a newspaper ad offering $4.50? Granted, it was the '60s, but please ... think about it!

The reason Dr. Milgram wanted to do these experiments in the first place was what he'd seen the people in Germany doing in response to Hitler's leadership. He was interested in answering a question that had haunted him from childhood: "What psychological mechanism transformed the average, and presumably normal, citizens of Germany and its allies into people who would carry out or tolerate unimaginable acts of cruelty against their fellow citizens who were Jewish, resulting in the death of six million of them?" (Blass, 2004).

His interest in this led him to conduct experiments into obedience, and he set up a simulated shock-generator box that had a label on it that read, "SHOCK GENERATOR, TYPE ZLB,

DYSON INSTRUMENT COMPANY, WALTHAM, MASS OUTPUT 15 VOLTS – 450 VOLTS" (Blass, 2004, p. 79).

Initially, the "shocker" started giving a low voltage of what they believed was an actual shock, and they were then asked to gradually increase the voltage in response to suggestions from the experimenter, who would say things like:

1. Please continue.
2. The experiment requires that you continue.
3. It is absolutely essential that you continue.
4. You have no other choice, you must go on.

The experiment was intended to show just how far the "shocker" would go, based on receiving commands from someone in authority. This was all part of an experiment done at Yale. Predictions on how many people would be willing to continue to shock at high voltage levels were low ... about 3%. In actuality, however, 65% were willing to give them the juice at the maximum level. Only 1% of the participants in the experiment, after having learned that it had been fake, were sorry they had participated.

Milgram had the following to say about the results: "Ordinary people, simply doing their jobs, and without any particular hostility on their part, can become agents in a terrible destructive process. Moreover, even when the destructive effects of their work become patently clear, and they are asked to carry out actions incompatible with fundamental standards of morality, relatively few people have the resources needed to resist authority" (Milgram, 1974).

Milgram went out of his way to ensure that this simulation looked real. He wanted those doing the shocking to believe they had actually caused the person receiving the voltage pain. Those receiving the fake jolts would emit pitiful screams, begging the person to stop shocking them. "The obedience experiments presented a disturbing view of human behavior. Milgram, his colleagues, and later the public were surprised by the sheer power of an authority to compel someone to hurt an innocent person, despite the absence of any coercive means to back up his commands" (Blass, 2004, p. 93).

What does this say about our personalities? Think about Dwight Shrute on the TV show *The Office*? Isn't he willing to do just about anything that Michael tells him to do to please his boss or, in other words, a person of authority? We've all worked alongside the Dwights of the world. Is it Michael who is to blame for how Dwight acts because he takes advantage of his willingness to please? Possibly.

How do you keep from turning into Dwight? How are you supposed to question your boss? In hard economic times such as we have experienced recently, many people find it difficult to turn down any request at work. Fear of losing one's job is a big factor in what we will allow. Unfortunately, many may not feel as if they have a choice, and will comply with demands. Is it OK to never question authority? There comes a point when employees feel psychologically abused, whether they recognize it or not. When someone is constantly a target of abuse of authority, they may not realize what's happening right away. One instance of someone in authority making a negative comment may go unnoticed, however, should the comments continue, that can constitute an abuse of authority. This abuse can lead to poor work performance as the employee's self-esteem drops.

Think of how self-esteem tied into Emotional Intelligence in Chapter 3. Part of having a high EQ was to have high levels of self-esteem. If we're allowing ourselves to be intimidated by those with authority on a constant basis, it can weaken our level of self-esteem, which can in turn lead to poor productivity.

Intimidation can come not only from our superiors, but also from our peers. We're now talking about bullying in the workplace. You think you get past the bullies of your youth, only to find that the SOBs show up at work in adulthood as well. One is considered to be bullied when other individuals or groups of individuals try to intimidate them or make them feel that their safety is at risk. This is usually due to a misuse of power, and the person who is being bullied may feel defenseless.

How can bullying affect one's personality? People can develop both physical and mental health problems as a result of bullying, including becoming stressed, requiring time off, leading to financial problems, having difficulty sleeping, and becoming physically ill with headaches, stomach aches or other stress-related illnesses. Keep in mind that bullying is not the same as harassment. Harassment is when unwelcomed conduct affects a person's employment. Bullying is not illegal, and may not even be recognized by the person who is being bullied.

Part of overcoming bullying is recognizing it and realizing that it's someone else's fault for bullying you, and not yours for getting bullied. It's a good idea to document what's occurring, so that you have a paper trail of evidence. Hopefully, employers will have a policy of zero tolerance for such activities. Many companies have HR departments that you can contact for help. If you see someone getting bullied, it might be a good idea to pull that person aside and talk to them as a friend, so they don't feel alone. You never know what might make that person flip. Who knows, you might have a Milton in your office, who will set the building on fire because he didn't get his stapler back. Gotta love the movie *Office Space* ... but seriously, it could happen!

One of the most effective ways to deal with difficult people is to try and listen more. Sometimes, you may not be hearing what they are saying to you through their bullying. Perhaps you are being bullied because you said or did something to piss someone off, and are not aware of it. Remember to avoid talking about controversial subjects that may be upsetting to others.

Some topics that you definitely want to avoid at work include:

1. Religion
2. Politics
3. Sex
4. How much money you make
5. Personal life and problems
6. Spreading gossip
7. Talking behind the boss's back, or anyone's back for that matter
8. Complaints about work
9. Your wild weekend
10. Your opinion of how people look, dress, or act.

Think about when you were in high school. Remember how caddy everyone acted? People would gossip, spread rumors, and share secrets. I'm sure each and every one of you has heard a nasty rumor spread about you, or found out so and so was talking behind your back. Or maybe you might even be the Regina George from the movie *Mean Girls*, the one actually doing the gossiping. Well, you'd better knock it off, or karma might take over and you'll get hit by a giant bus and break your neck, just like Regina did in the movie.

But seriously, our high school days have haunted us enough, and so wouldn't it be nice not to have to go through round two of the drama now that high school is over? Well, we're sorry to say, it doesn't change much as you get older and enter the workplace. People still like to talk. Remember, if someone is telling you something about someone else, you can assume that they're talking about you to someone else as well. Even if you trust this person, it might be better to politely tell them you'd rather not gossip about coworkers. This will save you from being dragged into an unwanted situation should things escalate. Plus, we all deal with enough drama outside of work, so dealing with it 24/7 can get a little tiresome. Aren't we going to work to get our jobs done, rather than to relive high school again?

Even if you keep your own mouth shut, you can still run into people at work who can make your life miserable. If someone is argumentative, be sure to apologize and say you're sorry they feel the way they do. Being combative doesn't usually help. That doesn't mean you should let them walk all over you, though. It's important to keep a positive attitude. Sometimes, killing the bad guy with kindness actually works, because it can disarm them. Some people are just looking for a fight, and if you give it to them, you'll continue to have more battles down the road. Sometimes, you may be tempted to over-react. When you find yourself upset by what someone has said, take a break and cool off.

Think of that stupid email you sent someone when you were in a bad mood. It came back to bite you later, right? Nothing is worse than putting something in writing that makes you look like a jerk. What you should put in writing, however, is any documentation to support your case in the event that things get out of hand, because you may need it to save your job. However, don't be too paranoid and trigger-happy. Put away your defense weapon for a minute, in this case your #2 pencil you're using to write down each allegation of bullying against your co-worker. Just because Suzy in Marketing didn't agree with your marketing idea doesn't mean she's being a bully, or trying to battle you. There are certain things that constitute bullying or intentional intimidation, so what we're saying is, keep that pencil handy, and only jot down recurring instances or situations that would be exceedingly apparent to everyone else. Constant tattletaling isn't necessary. In the end, only you can decide what crosses the line, and what is sufficient to really have a negative effect on you at work.

What is important in relation to job satisfaction is the realization that you have to create it yourself. Part of being happy at work is finding that thing that you love to do, which can be difficult when you're young. Part of getting to the level of employment that you hope to attain is surviving the lower levels that may not be so much fun. To find your own power, you need to understand your skills and preferred behaviors. Part of having power is creating it yourself.

How do you create power and find happiness at work? A lot of it comes from having high expectations of yourself. If you're just doing the minimum, you're not truly investing yourself in your work. Don't just simply look at the job description for what you need to accomplish, but rather think about what you can do above and beyond that in order to flourish. Think of all your coworkers who make that mistake. If you've ever uttered the words "It's not in my job description", you're definitely missing the boat! By going the extra mile, volunteering, helping others by sharing your skills and sharing the load, you'll not only feel good about yourself, but will also gain skills that will eventually catapult you further along in your career.

What other things can help to make you happy at work? Here are 10 things you can do that, according to YES! Magazine, that have been proven by scientists, will make you happy:

1. Smile
2. Take Initiative
3. Have Goals
4. Savor Every Day
5. Make Friends
6. Devalue Money
7. Give Away Something to Someone
8. Avoid Comparisons
9. Say Thank You
10. Exercise

Think about it. You can do most of these things at work. We don't recommend bringing your workout equipment into work, but short of that, many of these things are doable. One of the most important things on this list is the need to have goals. We recommend you have both personal and work-related goals established ... and written down. "In 1964, all members of the Harvard Business School graduating class stated that they have, at graduation, clear goals that they want to accomplish in life. Among them, 5% took the time to write it down on paper. In 1984, a follow-up study was done and it was discovered that 95% of those who wrote down their goals were able to achieve them within 20 years. Among the "lazy" majority, only 5% of them were able to reach their expected goals" (Fitzvillafuerte. com, 2010).

You might think you have goals, and perhaps you do have some vague idea of what you want to do with your life, but part of having power in your life is having direction. The oft-quoted line by Yogi Berra says it all: "If you don't know where you are going, you will wind up somewhere else." Perhaps one of your goals was to improve your personality, or at least understand it. If so, congratulations! By reading this book, you're well on your way to achieving your goal.

The most important part of setting goals is to not only write them down, but to also have specific timeframes and details to make them measurable. Having goals is having power! There are so many people in the world who seem to just exist and float along. They get up, they go to work, they go home, and they go to bed. The next day, they repeat the cycle. They're not living ... they're merely existing. By creating a plan and a map for your life, you won't fall into that category. Rather, you'll truly live your life to the full.

'What kinds of goals should I have?' you may be thinking. It's all about what is most important to you individually, but there are several key areas that you should consider:

- Career
- Family
- Education
- Health
- Financial

Part of understanding your personality is deciding what it is that's important to you. Where do you want to go in life? Do you have a path you are following? By creating goals, you're creating that pathway. All of these areas of your life are equally important, and each one should have goals that you work towards achieving. Do you really want to be in the job you're in right now for the next 20 years? We're guessing not, or at least not the same position. Take control of your life and create your future, basing it upon your personality and your dreams.

Let's look at an example of a goal. Suppose you want to get that promotion at work that requires a Bachelor's Degree. You might simply say that you'll get your degree. But is that all you have to do to set up a goal? Unfortunately, that won't do much for you. When will you get it? How will you get it? These questions haven't been answered yet, and until you answer these questions, your goal is just hanging out there in space. Chances are, that's where it will stay. If you don't set up guidelines and expectations of yourself, you may never attain your goal.

The first thing you have to do is write down a reasonable timeframe in which you will obtain your degree. Let's say you want to complete it in four years. Great. In your calendar, or planner, or simply on a piece of paper – heck, even on your bathroom mirror – write down the date by which you will attain this goal. Next, you need to break your goal down into smaller steps. Start at the end, and work backwards to what you need to do now. For example, to end up with a degree in four years time, you'll need to take certain classes in years 1, 2, 3, and 4. Now you need to set out those classes in writing. For example, in year 1 you may need to take English 101 and Algebra. In year 2, you may need to take more advanced courses, etc. Now, work backwards some more. How will you pass the first of these courses? You need to write down the specific steps that you will need to take on a monthly, weekly or even daily basis. For example, you might write down that you will study every Monday, Tuesday, and Wednesday from 6 pm to 7 pm, you will review the following week's homework requirements every

Sunday night at 7 pm, and you will get a tutor for the dreaded Statistics course, etc. Now, move even further backwards, all the way to the beginning, or "now". You might write down something like, 'I will go to the community college on Monday at 5 pm to sign up for classes.' You need to get very specific here, and make all goals measurable, so that you can mark them off your list as you complete them. Yes, we know, this sounds like a lot of work, having to write each step out in detail, but trust us, if you want to achieve your goals, this is the best way to start.

CHAPTER 7:
COLOR TESTS

*"In order to have friendship, you must look past the **color** to the soul, because with the soul lies a rainbow of many **colors**."*

— Anonymous

If you have taken any personality tests in the past, chances are one of them included dividing personalities into different color groups. There are several companies who offer these types of assessments, but one example is a test called Management by Strengths. This particular test was given at a company where Diane worked at one point. At this company, you were required to take the test and then display your results proudly on the wall of your cubicle. The company felt very strongly about the importance of understanding each other's personalities, and so it was explained to us that by posting your results on your work space, you were telling your coworkers how you preferred to be treated. Their hope was that, by increasing employees' understanding of each other, they would not only increase productivity but also improve morale and help with customer satisfaction.

Management by Strengths (MBS) assigns people to one of four color categories; Red, Green, Blue, or Yellow. Most people have a little bit of each of the colors, but usually, one color or a combination of colors is dominant. Results are broken down into a chart that shows one's preference for each of the four areas. Here's what the various colors signify.

Red: Those with a high Red score can tend to be control freaks. They are very direct, speak their mind, and sometimes hurt people's feelings in the process. They can be natural problem-solvers, and exude a lot of confidence, but this confidence sometimes comes across as having a large ego. They don't like to be micro-managed. Many sales managers are Reds. They like to take control and, having been in sales, have learned to be very direct.

Green: Those with a high Green rating tend to be extroverts. They are people persons, the talkative, friendly, enthusiastic person who does well working on teams. They like to be involved, but don't mind delegating. They come across as very cheerful, but they can also get their feelings hurt easily if scolded. We are both high-rating Greens.

Blue: Those with a high Blue score may work at a slower pace, and come across as calm and cooperative. Don't rush a Blue though, because it will drive them nuts. They may seem like they have a long fuse, but if it blows, watch out! This doesn't happen often though, and in general they come across as easy-going. When working with a Blue, give them a heads up on things and be sure that they have plenty of time so that they aren't rushed.

Yellow: Those with a high Yellow rating are all about structure. This is the guy who likes to read the entire manual before using his new cell phone. They don't want to make a mistake, so they're very organized, and like to check and double-check everything. Make sure you spell out the rules to these people, because they like instructions. Diane's husband, Toni's step-dad, is definitely a Yellow. That's why he's a doctor. Many people with a high Yellow rating become doctors and engineers.

What is interesting is that there tends to be a similar number of people falling into each of the four color areas overall. We're not just one color, however. We're all some combination of all four colors, with one of them standing out among the others. Diane rates highest in the area of Green, but she also has a high Red, a low Blue, and a really low Yellow rating. We all have at least a little bit of each of these color traits.

The advantage of knowing all this about your coworkers is a better understanding of each other's communication style. The thinking is that the more you know about someone, the more effectively you can work together. According to the MBS people, the benefits of their program are such that participants will:

- Learn to focus on those around you to improve communication, production and profits.
- Achieve greater self-understanding through the analysis of your own profile.
- Understand how to identify and capitalize on the strengths of employees.
- Resolve interpersonal conflicts that are usually rooted in misunderstanding.
- Reduce costly turnover that results when employees are dealt with the wrong way.
- Teach your people how to support each other.
- Improve your interviewing skills so that you hire the right employee for your organization.
- Avoid losing sales due to salesmen overselling the deal.

- Enhance your personal life through a deeper understanding of your family.
- Become more effective at closing by identifying your customer's decision-making style.
- Discover how to motivate rather than de-motivate your employees.
- Understand why a salesman's "style" may be turning off 3/4 of potential customers.
- See that a direct and candid suggestion is not meant as criticism.
- Learn steps to implement change with people that are "set in their ways."
- Learn simple yet very effective ways to reduce stress in your life.
- Increase customer satisfaction and "stand out" among your competition.
- Learn how to get referrals from every deal.

Clinical psychologists, including Dr. Nick Carden from the Renaissance Center of Albany, have reviewed this program. Dr. Carden compared MBS to our old friend the MBTI and found that the MBS was more user-friendly, had a more practical application, was dependable, and had good implementation possibilities in the workplace. However, the validity and test construction was stronger for the MBTI.

Another use for the MBS is to enable you to better understand your customers. Let's say you're in sales. You might be a Blue calling on a Red. Your preference is to go slow, and be relaxed and easy-going, which is going to drive the Red customer crazy! She wants you to get to the point. No putzing around with what you have to say ... just spit it out! It's important to adjust your personality to fit those you're working with.

Now suppose you're a Red calling on a Blue customer. You may rush in and demand what you want, with no apologies. This is going to freak the Blue customer out. They need time to make decisions and think about what they want to do. They need for you to be more patient with them, and to listen to what their needs are.

Suppose you're a Green calling on a Yellow. Greens are used to talking away and interrupting the conversation, such as it is, with whatever comes into their mind at any given point in time. A Yellow, however, is not interested in all that stuff. They simply want the facts, and love to ask "why?" If you want them to buy from you, you need to spell out exactly what's in it for them, and then sit patiently as they write out all their notes.

What if you're a Yellow calling on a Green? Well, the Green may not be terribly impressed with all your technical manuals. They want to talk about things that you may not have planned on talking about in the first place. The product that you have spent days compiling research on may now not even be the product they are interested in. You'll have to be ready to switch gears and talk it all out with them.

How can this MBS survey discover all this information about people? Asking you to rate, on a scale of 1–5, how useful you think certain words are in describing yourself determines what color you are. There are other tests that Diane has had to take in order to get through job interviews that were similar. Sometimes, these tests have you rate how you see yourself, and also how you think others see you. The MBS is mostly about how you see yourself.

MBS is not the only color-based personality test out there, indeed there are several. Another popular one is the

Hartman Personality Profile, also known as The Color Code, created by Dr. Taylor Hartman. In his book *The People Code*, Dr. Hartman defines personality as "that core of thoughts and feelings inside you that tells you how to conduct yourself. It's a checklist of responses based on strongly held values and beliefs. It directs you to respond emotionally and rationally to every life experience" (2007, p. 13). In his book, he also divides people into four color groups:

Red: These would be the power wielders. These people tend to be very logical and determined. You will probably find a lot of leaders are Reds. They may come across as unemotional and task-driven. They are determined to succeed. Like the Reds in the MBS profile, their directness may come across as lacking tact at times. This can also make them seem demanding. If Reds need to work on something, it probably is compassion.

Blue: These would be the do-gooders. Blues are all about intimacy and connecting with humanity. They have a strong purpose and are very loyal and dependable. Maybe they call them Blue because they tend to be more moody and can be worriers. They are tenacious though and don't quit until the job is done. Sometimes that means hanging onto something that they should have given up a long time ago. Blues require a lot of appreciation from you. Don't ignore a Blue if you ever want them to be on your side in the future.

White: These are the peace keepers. Whites are patient and non-judgmental people. They show a lot of tact and don't rock the boat. If you want to go crying to someone about your problems, they are good listeners. They don't tend to show their problems to you however. Whites tend to avoid change and have a problem with setting long term goals for some lack foresight.

Yellow: These are the fun lovers. Yellows just want to have fun ... or is that girls? Well, apparently both Yellows and girls do. The Yellows are the enthusiastic optimists of the world. It was probably a Yellow who wrote "Don't Worry, Be Happy." They can be very charming and enjoy being around people. Because they are overly optimistic, they may overlook reality and not see that something bad is actually happening. At their worst, they may seem self-centered because they are always looking for the best friend and the best time at the expense of leaving those who don't fall into those categories behind.

As with the MBS color test, The Color Code assigns a primary color but also a secondary color to your personality. For example, in both of these color tests, you may be highest in the Red category but you may also have a high Green, or some other color. Everyone has different levels of each of the colors in color tests. According to Hartman, we are basically the color that our personality shows from taking the test. We may try to change, but we are innately the person that the results reveal.

Why is it so important to understand our personalities and how they relate to others? Hartman claims that, "This year 85 percent of the employees who lose their jobs will lose them because of personality conflicts. Only 15 percent will lose their jobs because they lack technical expertise" (2007, p. 147). According to his system, there are different interactions to be aware of between various combinations of color types. For example putting two Blues together may just create a perfect fit, two Whites will tolerate each other well, and two Reds placed together can be very dynamic. One of the things about taking this type of personality test that differs from taking a MBTI or DiSC (which we will discuss later) is that it is more about why we act the way we do, and not about our preferences.

If you're interested in taking a free version of this test, check out http://www.colorcode.com/personality_test/. Not surprisingly, Diane's results showed that she was 53% Red. As you may recall, Reds are motivated by power. They can also be workaholics, types, Diane, as she works away endlessly! On the other hand, Toni turned out to be a Yellow. She's always been on the fun-loving side.

CHAPTER 8:
CONCERN FOR IMPACT

"Nothing in the world is more dangerous than a sincere ignorance and conscientious stupidity."

— Martin Luther King, Jr.

What is Concern for Impact? If you try to look up books about Concern for Impact, chances are you won't find any with that title. This is a term that encompasses a lot of different things that many authors have tried to address in some detail. Basically, what it includes are a lot of different factors that make up how much you care about what others think about you.

You have undoubtedly heard the expression "first impressions". People can and do size other people up when they first meet them. We may think we know their character just by looking at their expressions, their stance, their gestures, etc. Sometimes, however, what comes across as a personality issue may just be situational. Maybe they're having a bad day, but we've probably made a preliminary judgment about them in our minds regardless.

We've all met the guy or gal who just doesn't care what others think about them. These people have a low Concern for Impact. They see the world from a narcissistic viewpoint. Unfortunately, in the business world, they make it difficult for everyone else to function successfully. However, we're sure these people care at least a little bit about what others think about them, and are probably just putting on this "I don't give a darn" act. It's human nature to be concerned about what others think about us.

In order to be successful in life, it is important to know how we make other people feel. We like to be around people who make us feel good about ourselves, and part of getting what we want from people is giving them what they want. "The more you listen and connect, the more likely it is that others will return the attention. A first interaction may be an opportunity for two people to experience a pleasant moment, or it may be the start of a friendship, social connection, business relationship or romance" (Demarais and White, 2004, p. 25).

You may be wondering what good it is to know about this. What you can do, as a co-worker, to change these people? Well, we're sorry to say, you probably can't change them. You can, however, influence how they react to you simply by maintaining a pleasant mood, which can be infectious. On the other hand, if you exude negativity, others can easily feed off this emotion, leading to an unconstructive or even toxic atmosphere. We all know the term "misery loves company." Your bad mood can drag others down.

You can also learn to work around the Negative Nancys in the workplace based on understanding that, unfortunately, this is the way they are, and figuring out ways not to be sucked in to the negativity. You can also try to figure out if you are one of these people who lack Concern for Impact, and if so, try to work on your own faults as well. Think of having a lack of Concern for Impact as like having body odor. You may not be able to smell yourself, but others are nearly passing out or secretly spraying you with Axe body spray as you walk past.

What types of things make up Concern for Impact? Here's a list of the top ten things you may need to work on, or may need to recognize in others, so you can alter the way you communicate with them:

1. Tone
2. Expressions
3. How you word things
4. Eye contact
5. How do others describe you
6. Fidgetiness
7. Annoying laughs or other sounds
8. Opinionated
9. Overly religious or pushy about ideas
10. Depressed or negative

When you hear the word 'tone', what do you think of? Tone of voice? Well, that's part of it. Do you have an annoyed tone when you speak to people? Do you sound like you're in a rush? Maybe you sound bored or disengaged. A person's tone conveys a lot about them. Think about your friends on Facebook; they use their voice or tone in words that they write. Look at a few of the status updates they've posted. Are they negative? Are they positive? Are they a combination? Those may be the most confusing. If they say something like "Yesterday sucked but I'm hoping today will be better," that's more positive than "Yesterday was good but today will probably suck." However, both of these messages send a negative message to some extent. Do you want to be that negative person? Do you post negative outgoing comments? If so, you might not realize it, but your tone is coming through loud and clear to everyone else.

Eventually, people are going to get tired of hearing your negativity, and will seek to avoid you. That's how it is at work as well.

We heard of a story where the people at one workplace nicknamed a fellow employee "Eeyore" from *Winnie the Pooh* because of the tone of his voice. He doesn't know he's been given this nickname, and he probably doesn't even realize that he's perceived this way. Usually, he isn't even down, or in a bad mood – it's just the monotonous sound of his voice that caused them to coin this nickname for him. It's draining just to talk to him.

Let's face it, work is not always the most fun thing we do in our day, but if you have that annoying co-worker next to you complaining about how difficult their job is or how much they'd rather be fishing, it only makes things worse. If you are that co-worker who talks about where they'd rather be or what they'd rather be doing, then stop it! You're driving everyone around you crazy and bringing down the energy in the place.

If you're around someone who does this, there are a few things you can do. One is to point out to them that they're being a pain, but then you risk hurting their feelings or pissing them off. Another thing you can do is totally avoid them, so that you don't have to listen to their negativity, but that could be a difficult option if your desks are practically touching, or they're your immediate cubicle neighbor. Maybe the best solution if you're forced to work with these people is to point out some good things whenever they say something negative. Or, when they finally do say something positive, react strongly with positive words about what they just said. We talked earlier about how nowadays people like affirmation, and to be rewarded. By rewarding that person with praise for the positive comment they made, you make it more likely that they'll continue to be more positive.

For example, should they complain that it's Monday again, you can respond in a positive manner to shut them up. Try saying something like, "Yeah, but I had so much fun this weekend, I needed to get back to work so I could actually feel productive and not just be recuperating in bed all day." If you continue to say something positive in response to their negative comments, hopefully they'll have enough sense to see what you're doing, and stop their negativity around you.

Tone doesn't always just mean complaining negativity, either. It can also be a sarcastic or rude demeanor. Dr. Zachary Smith has been quoted as saying, "Sarcasm is the recourse of the weak mind," and he has a point. How hard is it to make something sound sarcastic? It usually doesn't take a lot of wit. We have known some people who can really pull it off, though, in fact Diane had one boss who was great at it, and knew just when it was appropriate. However, it can be very draining to be around sarcastic people when they don't have a knack for it. Have you noticed that people who use constant sarcasm usually find themselves undeniably hysterical while the rest of the world might just be rolling their eyes? You don't want to be that person. That's not to say that an occasional sarcastic comment with an accompanying smile can't be a little fun or cute, but don't overdo it, or it just becomes annoying and rude, especially in the workplace. It's one of the best ways to be seen as truly anti-social.

Here are some sarcastic quotes, just to give you an idea of things that others have said to piss people off:

I feel so miserable without you, it's almost like having you here.
- Stephen Bishop

I didn't like the play, but then again I saw it under adverse conditions ... the curtain was up.
- Groucho Marx

He is a self-made man and worships his creator.
- Irvin S. Cobb

He has Van Gogh's ear for music.
- Billy Wilder

Every time I look at you I get a fierce desire to be lonesome.
- Oscar Levant

While sarcasm can be very funny at times, it has to be kept to a minimum at work. If you're around someone who is sarcastic, trying to outdo their sarcasm can only make things worse. If you're the one being sarcastic, this is another way you can be driving everyone crazy. To increase your Concern for Impact, watch how people react when you say something sarcastic. Are they cringing or giving you a semi-fake smile? Perhaps you aren't as funny as you think you are. Time to leave that up to the professional comedians, funny guy! Wait, were we just using sarcasm right there? Oops! Also, if it's someone else who's being sarcastic, sometimes it's best to point out that they've hurt your feelings, if that's the case. Many times, people don't realize they're being insulting. Sarcasm can become a bad habit for some, so try to recognize how often you tend to use sarcasm in your daily interactions with people, and quickly nip it in the bud if it's excessive.

Another important aspect of having Concern for Impact is to realize what your facial expressions are saying to other people. A cool new TV show called *Lie to Me* has really brought to light how much your expressions really tell the world what you are thinking. Vanderbilt University did a study that found that a person's face sticks in our mind more than other things about them. For a bit of fun, check out this link that lets you create a face that you find appealing: http://www.faceresearch.org/. This is a part of research showing that we are attracted or repelled by certain facial expressions.

Have you ever had someone come up to you and say something like, "It will get better ... cheer up"? Perhaps you looked depressed to them, although it could be just another dumb pick-up line, so watch out for those creepers! This reminds us of a really bad pick-up line a guy tried on one of us recently. He said, "I'm getting married Saturday. Would you like to be the bride?" We could do a whole book on pick-up lines you shouldn't use ... but we digress. The point is, your facial expression is something you need to be aware of. Other people are reacting to you based on what they see on your face.

Try this experiment at work. Walk around the workplace and look at the expressions everyone has on their face. Are they serious? Are they depressed? Are they happy? Sad? Chances are, if they have a positive expression, such as a happy or smiling face, you'll want to be around them more. Think about how others are viewing you. Do you look annoyed, tired, depressed, or bored? If so, do you really think that those people who are considering giving you a raise or promoting you aren't noticing? It's important to make a conscious effort to maintain an upbeat facial expression if you have any hopes of ever getting promoted. No one wants to promote the infamous eye roller, so knock that off right now if you're doing it!

Another important aspect of Concern for Impact is how you word things. Are you clear? Could your ideas be misinterpreted? This is another area where sarcasm could come into play. Remember that if you want to get along well with others at work, you must be sure that what you're trying to relay to others in terms of communication is effective. It's no secret that many of the problems at work are due to communication failures. When you try to communicate your ideas to your coworkers or your boss, do you follow up with questions to be sure they understand what you mean? If someone is communicating something to you that you don't understand, do you ask them to rephrase what they said so that you can better understand them? If you're not doing these things, there may be a communication breakdown.

How is your eye contact when you speak with other people? "Researchers investigated how much eye contact is typical in a face-to-face interaction. It turns out that most people make eye contact 45 to 60 percent of the time" (Demarais and White, 2004, p. 62). Have you ever talked to someone who is looking at the floor, or reading through something, or just looking at something else rather than looking you in the eye? How annoying is that? It makes them come across as if they have something to hide.

If you're guilty of this, you need to understand that it makes you look cold, or disinterested in the other person. However, that might actually be the case; maybe you aren't making eye contact for good reason. Maybe you're actually engaged in your work, and Mr. Blabbermouth is interrupting you to talk about his personal life. By not making eye contact, it shows you are busy or uninterested, and he should get the hint that you're trying to work. Studies have shown that those who make little eye contact "were perceived as more superficial, less socially attractive, and less credible than people who made an average or high eye contact" (Demarais and White, 2004, p. 62).

Eye contact is essential to show that you care about what is being said. If someone is not looking you in the eye, you might try saying something that's not too confrontational, but lets them know that they're not looking at you. Perhaps you could try something like, "Who's here? I noticed you were looking over there." Sometimes people don't realize that they're not looking at you, so by doing this, you can bring their attention back to the conversation. If enough people do this to these rude people, perhaps they'll get the message that they actually need to look at the person they're conversing with! On the flip side, maybe that person is trying to give you a hint that you're talking too much, and they're trying to work, and they're not interested in what you're talking about. By them not making eye contact, they may think you'll get the hint that they don't want to get engaged in your conversation, and want to be left alone. Make sure you can spot the differences.

Have you ever thought about how others would describe you? That might be an important question to ask yourself. Have you ever met a person who thinks they're God's gift to Earth, while everyone else thinks they're a jerk? In the movie *What Women Want*, Mel Gibson really thought that women adored him, until he heard what their voices in their heads were saying. When he found out what they really thought, he realized how obnoxious he really was.

Sometimes, it helps to write down words that you think others would use to describe you. One organization where Diane worked had a test as part of the initial job interview where you were given a bunch of words to choose from. On one side of the paper you had to write down the words you would use to describe yourself. On the other side of the paper, you had to write the words that you thought others would use to describe you. The company was interested in your metaperception. Say what? A person's metaperception is how they see themselves. Studies have shown that people with personality disorders may have trouble seeing themselves as others do. Even without a personality disorder, many of us fail to interpret how others perceive us. According to Psychology Today (2009), "Classic work by psychologist Paul Ekman has shown that most people can't tell when others are faking expressions. Who knows how many interactions you've walked away from thinking you were a hit while your new friend was actually faking agreeability?"

It has been shown that people who want to be liked may convince themselves that they were actually liked, when in fact they may not have been. If you're good at understanding how others perceive you, you're less likely to be that person who thinks they're funny, while the people around them are actually wincing in embarrassment for them.

Psychology Today ran an article that suggested we should do an exit interview on ourselves whenever a relationship does not work out well. Have you ever broken up with someone? Well, the experts feel that if you have, you might want to contact your ex and ask them to be painfully clear about the things you really need to change about your personality. It might be hard to hear, but it might be a real eye opener, and an opportunity for you to change things about yourself you might not even have been aware of.

One important thing we need to work on is self-awareness. This is part of having emotional intelligence (see Chapter 3). Have you ever watched yourself on a video? It can be very disturbing the first time you do it. We strongly recommend that you watch yourself a time or two while you're interacting with other people. Check out your mannerisms, your voice, and your attitude. How do you come across? Are you surprised by what you see? Have others watch the tape as well, and ask them to critique you. If you really want to be a success in the business world, ignorance may not be bliss. You may need accurate feedback to make some important, necessary changes.

Part of how you come across involves but your physical mannerisms. Are you fidgety, do you act nervous, or are there some distracting little things that you do? Being of Italian background, we both talk a lot with our hands. Some may see that as animated and charming, while others may find it distracting. When in the business-world setting, it's important to realize that overly exaggerated expressions or fidgeting can make others uncomfortable. If you're shaking your foot right now and don't realize it, you may be guilty of a few of these mannerisms, and you may want to work on eliminating them.

Noises are another issue. Just say the words 'annoying laugh' and the character Janice from *Friends* comes to mind. Imagine if you had to work next to that chick every day!? One of our favorite radio talk shows (Frosty, Heidi and Frank) has a girl on it with a laugh like a hyena. She's made it a sort of personal trademark, which may work well in the radio world, but in the real working world, something like that could cost you business, make people avoid you, or just drive everyone around you crazy.

Do people often mention something you do that's loud or annoying? If you've been told more than once that a noise you make stands out from the norm, you probably have an issue. Think of the line Meryl Streep delivered to Bruce Willis in the movie *Death Becomes Her*. At one point, she looked at him and said, "Can you just not breathe?" If you're a mouth-breather, or a cougher, or a sniffer, you might be driving those around you nuts without even knowing it.

It may not just be the bodily sounds that you make that are the problem. Are the words that are coming out of your mouth the issue? Are you overly opinionated? Do you love to talk about religion or politics? Those are the kinds of issues that are not necessarily going to endear you to others at all times. Do you assume that because you love Rush Limbaugh, Howard Stern or some other opinionated celebrity, everyone else does as well? You may be wrong.

Talking about things that no one else cares about may include talking too much about yourself. Are you a conversational narcissist? If you're noticing that people are trying to change the conversation a lot, you just may be one of these. "What makes a conversational narcissist? Psychologists have identified some key elements: Boasting, refocusing the topic of the conversation on the self, speaking in a loud voice, using "I" statements and inappropriately lengthy speech, and "glazing over" when others speak" (Demarais and White, 2004, p. 74).

Probably the most common thing that drives us crazy at work is the overly depressed or negative person. They'll suck the life right out of you. Are you that person? Do you constantly have something negative to say? Are you always saying you're tired, or you're over-worked, or you have problems with your girlfriend/boyfriend? If so, you probably don't realize how often you're doing it. Challenge yourself to spend a day paying attention to how many times you say something negative. Make a mark on a piece of paper every time you do. By pointing it out to yourself, you may be surprised just how natural it comes to you to complain. Complaining can be a bad habit, like anything else. You may simply need to retrain yourself to adopt a positive habit of only saying good things. You don't want to go overboard, however, and be that annoying person who answers the question "How are you doing" with "Great, but I'm getting better," but you can definitely bring the bad attitude up a few notches so that you aren't making others want to jump out of a window to avoid you.

Always keep in mind the impression you're making on others. One thing that many people overlook is how to keep pace with those who are listening to them. Some people prefer to listen at a faster pace, while others prefer a slower pace. If you're a fast talker, you probably prefer to listen to a fast talker, and vice versa. You will more likely appeal to those you're speaking to if you adjust your speed to match theirs.

Another important thing to remember is not to interrupt those who are speaking to you. That's a sure-fire way to let them know that you don't care what they're saying. Even if you really don't, it's better to fake it. Interestingly, when interrupting was studied, "Female listeners saw the interrupters negatively—as pushy, disrespectful, and unpleasant. Male listeners, however, had a more positive view of interrupters than women did. They were more likely to see the interrupters as expressing liking, interest and agreement" (Demarais and White, 2004, p. 143).

If we don't all agree on what is polite and what is offensive, how do you know how to respond to others? The best thing you can do is look for body language, and other clues. If they're looking away, or seem to be disengaging, it's time for you to make a change. The important thing is for you to be aware that your personality is impacting others, and so it's up to you to make the necessary adjustments based on the requirements of those with whom you're interacting.

CHAPTER 9:
ENNEAGRAM PROFILE

"Dwight has a big personality and I have a big personality and a lot of times when two people like that get together, it can be explosive."

— Phyllis from the TV show The Office

Another profiling test you may run across on the web is something called the Enneagram of Personality. Enneagram is Greek for 'nine things written,', and is pronounced ANY-a-gram. Along with this test, you would likely see a picture like this:

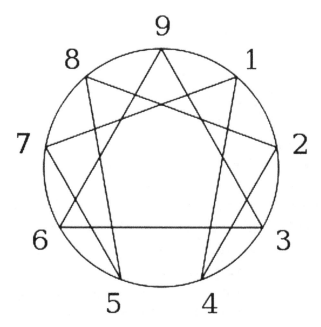

This symbol has been used in other areas of history and explanations of human nature, although the exact origin of it is not known. There are nine points on the circle, each of which represent a personality type. This personality test is referred to as the Riso-Hudson Enneagram Type Indicator, or RHETI, and is named after Don Richard Riso and Russ Hudson, who were the developers and leading teachers of the Enneagram system. Without going into too much detail, the circle can also be thought of as a kind of pie, wherein the numbers are divided into three separate slices. The numbers 2, 3, and 4 form one slice, 5, 6, and 7 form another, and 8, 9, and 1 make up the last slice. These three pieces of the pie are called Triads. It can get complicated, so for a more complete explanation, we recommend that you check out Riso's books. He currently has several best-selling books about personality types and the Enneagram system. For now, we'll explain what each of these nine number types mean.

Ones are the Reformers
Twos are the Helpers
Threes are the Achievers
Fours are the Individuals
Fives are the Investigators
Sixes are the Loyalists
Sevens are the Enthusiasts
Eights are the Challengers
Nines are the Peacemakers

Don Richard Riso has written a book, *Personality Types*, in which he discusses how to utilize this Enneagram for self-discovery. In the book, he addresses the importance of understanding personality types, although we probably didn't need to tell you that ... the title is pretty self-explanatory, right? He stated that, "It would be impossible for most of us to spend a day without coming into direct or indirect contact with dozens of people – family, friends, people on the street, at the office, on television, in our fantasies and fears. Our relationships with others are the most change-able, infuriating, pleasurable and mystifying elements in our lives" (p. 3). Riso has a very important point here in that we do not live in a vacuum. Therefore, we must learn how to understand ourselves, as well as those around us, in order to function in society. Part of this understanding comes from exploring personalities.

Let's take a look at these nine types that Riso has described to see what it means to be each one of these personali-ties. We'll begin with Type 1, or the Reformer. Someone with a good level in this personality profile has strong personal convictions, and may try to be fair and wise. The downside of this personality type is that they may become idealists and workaholics, and may be described as "anal" for being compulsive. Either way, this group strives to be correct and consistent. Some famous examples of a Type 1 are:

Harrison Ford
Spock from Star Trek
Al Gore

Type 2 personalities are the Helpers. Someone with a good level in this area might be seen as compassionate and empathetic. They're unselfish, and like to help others with their pursuits in life. At their worst in this profile, they may be seen as too much of a people-pleaser, wanting others to rely on them, and may even become possessive. If you work with someone who you feel may be trying to manipu-late you, this person would have an unhealthy level of the Type 2 Helper personality. Some famous examples of a Type 2 are:

Mother Teresa
Richard Simmons
Florence Nightingale

The Type 3 profile is the Motivator. Someone with strong levels in this area would probably been seen as someone with a lot of energy and self-esteem. They might come across as very authentic, because they are. These are the people who are going to be looking to run charities and be the silent Santa type. Those who may not have a good level of Type 3 would be more the social climber, someone who is more into the show of it all. They're more concerned about what people think about what they do, and may fear failure, therefore they exaggerate what they do to get people to think more highly of them. Some famous examples of Motivators are:

Richard Gere
Sting
Tom Cruise
Sharon Stone
Brooke Shields
Denzel Washington
Arnold Schwarzenegger
O. J. Simpson
Sylvester Stallone

The Type 4 profile is the Individualist. Someone who has good levels in this area is very self-aware. They may be seen as intuitive, as well as emotionally strong. These people can be very creative. Someone on the low end of this profile may become self-absorbed and moody. This is the person who likes to play the hard-to-get game. Some famous examples of the Individualist include:

Johnny Depp
Bob Dylan
Michael Jackson
Edgar Allan Poe

Type 5 is the Investigator. Someone with a good level of this profile may come across as curious, someone who notices their surroundings. They like to learn, and are very open-minded. They may be seen as pioneers. Someone with a low level here might come across as studious but detached, and possibly over-involved with their studies. They may not focus on reality, but instead on interpretations of what they believe is reality. Some famous examples of Investigators include:

Albert Einstein
Gary Larson
Stephen King
Stephen Hawking
Tim Burton
Vincent van Gogh

Type 6 profiles are the Loyalists. Someone who excels in this area may view trust as very important. They have foresight, and are hardworking, possibly self-sacrificing. They may seem independent, and yet they are also cooperative, positive thinkers. Someone who does not excel in this area may be seen as someone who is always looking for commit-ments (both the giving and receiving of). They like guide-lines, but don't like to be given a lot of demands, and may be procrastinators. At the worst level, they may become alcoholics due to their self-destructive behaviors. Some famous examples of this type include:

Tom Hanks
Bruce Springstein

Patrick Swayze
Princess Diana
Jay Leno
Julia Roberts
Woody Allen
Marilyn Monroe
Rush Limbaugh

Type 7 profiles are the Enthusiasts. This profile may be considered close to the Myers–Briggs Extrovert. They are talkative, invigorating, and spontaneous at high levels. They may also show a deep appreciation for what they have in their lives. Those with low levels may be seen as uninhibited, and may be prone to over-exaggeration and clowning around. They may even become juvenile in their actions or, at worst, abusive. Some famous examples of this group include:

Steven Spielberg
Robin Williams
Jim Carrey
Bette Midler
Elton John
Bruce Willis
Joan Rivers
Howard Stern

Type 8 is the Leader personality. At its best, this personality comes across as very self-confident and resourceful. This is the guy who makes decisions, and knows that he can do just about anything. They may seem courageous because of this, and may actually end up being a hero. At the lowest level, these people may come across as denying their own emotions, and be overly dominant. This may be the boss who is overly boastful and egocentric. You don't want to argue with them, because they may become belligerent. Some famous examples include:

Marlon Brando
Barbara Walters
Donald Trump
Martin Luther King, Jr.
Frank Sinatra
Saddam Hussein

The Type 9 personality is the Peacemaker. At their best, these people are very stable and accepting, and may come across as serene. They can be good communicators and mediators, and are good at developing relationships. At their worst, they may become overly accommodating to avoid of not getting along. They like peace, so they may walk away from facing their problems. They may even develop depression, and look to block out the negatives by becoming numb. Some famous examples of this type include:

Marge Simpson
Walt Disney
George Lucas
Kevin Costner
Keanu Reeves
Woody Harrelson
Ringo Starr
Whoopi Goldberg
Janet Jackson

One reason for learning Riso's profiles is to be able to work on understanding how our personalities work, and how these dominant parts of us integrate with other parts of our personality. By understanding how our types integrate, we can better avoid conflict, and work to have the best of all of those types of our personality.

CHAPTER 10:
STRONG INTEREST INVENTORY

"All I need is my brains, my eyes and my personality, for better or for worse."

— William Albert Allard

Because we're discussing personality tests in the work setting, we would be remiss not to mention the Strong Interest Inventory. This test helps with career assessment. "The Strong Interest Inventory assessment is one of the most widely used measures of vocational interest in the United States. It has been used in educational settings, public institutions, and private organizations for nearly 80 years" (Donnay et al., 2004, p. 2). Developed by E. K. Strong Jr. in 1927, this test has been revised several times and now includes 192 items on its inventory.

Don't worry, we won't list all 192 items! The questions are designed to discover your interests, and your scores assign you to one of six codes created by psychologist John Holland. You are given certain words or phrases to choose from depending on how strongly you relate to them, and the computer-analyzed results assign you to a scale. Your responses are then compared with those of other people in different types of occupations. The end result is supposed to tell you what type of occupation you would find the most rewarding. This assessment is designed to enable you to learn about job satisfaction or dissatisfaction (whether you're in the right or wrong job based on your personality), and has nothing to do with abilities; it's only about your interests. Diane talks about how you can change your career based upon your interests in her book *How to Reinvent Your Career*. If you're considering a change in careers, you should check it out.

The test is set up so that you can answer the various questions by responding with Strong Like, Like, Dislike or Strongly Dislike. Because this test is useful in determining work interests, some recent changes have been made to incorporate changes in the workplace. "The conventional theme, for example, was expanded to include programming and working with software, while the realistic theme was broadened to include working with computer hardware" (Donnay et al., 2004, p. 3). Some items from the original test haven't really changed through the years, though. These areas include such things as interest in athletics, science, math, culinary arts, and sales.

According to Holland, the personality can be related to the work environment, so that everyone can be classified into one of the following groups:

- **Realistic** – practical, physical, hands-on, tool-oriented
- **Investigative** – analytical, intellectual, scientific, explorative
- **Artistic** – creative, original, independent, chaotic
- **Social** – cooperative, supporting, helping, healing/ nurturing
- **Enterprising** – competitive environments, leadership, persuading
- **Conventional** – detail-oriented, organizing, clerical

A lot of these personality tests seem to have a cute geometric shape that goes along with them, and this one is no different. Holland assigned the following graphic to this test:

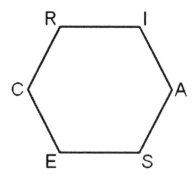

Each one of the six letters corresponds to the six different areas of personality that are observed. Based on these results, the subject can see which type of career they are most suited to. What follows is a list of careers that go along with the test results:

Do'er (Realistic) (R):

Those with a high level of R are all about building and repairing. Many find happiness in outdoor jobs. Diane tells her students not to cite Wikipedia as a source on papers, due to its ability to be manipulated. However, it can sometimes contain reliable information. Many of the jobs listed on Wikipedia on the basis of the Strong Interest Inventory were accurate. For example, the following are sample jobs that go along with the Realistic theme:

- Agriculture
- Archaeology
- Architect
- Astronaut
- Athlete
- Chef

- Computer science
- Driver
- Electrical engineering
- Engineer
- Firefighter
- Gardener
- Information technology
- Instructional technology
- Martial arts
- Mechanic/Automobiles
- Mechanical engineering
- Paramedic
- Pharmacy
- Physical therapy
- Pilot
- Veterinarian
- Police Officer
- Soldier

People can be a combination of themes. For example, they may not be totally R, or Realistic, but may be a combination of RI, or RS, or even RSI, etc. Keep reading, and you'll learn about these other themes. According to the technical manual: Strong Interest Inventory . . . Applications and Technical Guide by Harmon et al, the following are typical R-themed items of interest:

- Auto mechanic
- Electronics Technician
- Agriculture
- Clock Repair
- Popular Mechanics Magazine

Thinker (Investigative) (I):

The thinker enjoys working with theory and information, and is analytical, intellectual, scientific. The following are some sample jobs that go along with the Thinker theme:

- Actuary
- Computer science
- Economist
- Engineer
- Finance
- Lawyer
- Mathematics
- Pharmacy
- Physician/Medical school
- Professor (all fields)
- Psychologist
- Psychiatrist
- Science
- Statistics
- Surgeon

According to Harmon's technical manual, the following are typical I-themed items of interest:

- Author of technical books
- Chemistry
- Mathematics
- Zoology
- Research work

Creator (Artistic) (A):

The A-themed, or Artistic, person is non-conforming, original, independent, chaotic, creative. The following are some sample jobs that go along with the Artistic theme:

- Actor/Performance
- Animation
- Art therapy
- Artist
- Author/ Poet
- Dance therapy
- Expressive therapy
- Graphic designer
- Library and information science
- Music therapy
- Musician
- Painter

According to Harmon's technical manual, the following are typical A-themed items of interest:

- Author of novels
- Interior decorator
- Literature
- Symphony concerts
- Magazines about art or music

Helper (Social) (S):

The Social-themed person likes cooperative environments, supporting, helping, healing/nurturing. The following are sample jobs that go along with the Social theme:

- Art therapy
- Audiologist
- Babysitter
- Caretaker
- Counselor
- Dance therapy
- Education
- Instructional technology
- Martial arts
- Music therapy
- Nurse
- Nutritionist
- Physician
- Professor
- Psychologist
- Social Work
- Teacher
- Theology
- Trainer (Industry)
- Speech-Language Pathologist
- Occupational Therapist

According to Harmon's technical manual, the following are typical S-themed items of interest:

- High school teacher
- Social Worker
- Special education teacher
- Helping others overcome their difficulties
- Taking care of children

Persuader (Enterprising) (E):

The Enterprising theme prefers a competitive environment, leading, persuading, selling, dominating, promoting, status.

We would both be considered Persuaders. The following are sample jobs that go along with the Persuader theme:

- Administration
- Academic administration
- Business/MBA
- Communications
- Insurance
- Investment Banker
- Journalism
- Law/Politics
- Marketing/Advertising
- Management
- Management Consultant
- Public Health
- Publishing
- Public relations
- Public policy
- Real Estate
- Retail
- Stockbroker
- Salesmen

According to Harmon's technical manual, the following are typical E-themed items of interest:

- Auto salesperson
- Sales Manager
- Stockbroker
- Customer service representative
- People who have made fortunes in business

Organizer (Conventional) (C):

The Conventional-themed person tends to prefer being precise, perfect attention to detail, orderly, organizing, status. The following are sample jobs that go along with the Conventional theme:

- Accountant
- Actuary
- Administration
- Academic administration
- Banking/ Investment bank
- Business/MBA
- Clerk
- Copy Editing
- Instructional technology
- Payroll
- Proofreader
- Receptionist
- Retail
- Secretary
- Technical writer

According to Harmon's technical manual, the following are typical C-themed items of interest:

- Cashier in a bank
- Private secretary
- Statistician
- Financial analyst
- Developing business systems

The STRONG results should give the test taker an idea of what types of occupations they would prefer. Not all of them require a degree, in fact about 40% of the jobs that are listed don't require one. The following are occupations Harmon lists as not requiring degrees:

- Agribusiness Manager
- Auto mechanic
- Bookkeeper
- Carpenter
- Chef
- Child Care Provider
- Credit Manager
- Dental Assistant
- Dental Hygienist
- Electrician
- Emergency Medical Technician
- Farmer
- Flight Attendant
- Florist
- Food Service Manager
- Gardener/Groundskeeper
- Hair Stylist
- Horticultural Worker
- Housekeeping & Maintenance Supervisor
- Life Insurance Agent
- Medical Records Technician
- Medical Technician
- Military Enlisted Personnel
- Nurse, LPN
- Optician
- Paralegal
- Photographer
- Plumber
- Police Officer

- Purchasing Agent
- Radiologic Technologist
- Realtor
- Respiratory Therapist
- Restaurant Manager
- Secretary
- Small Business Owner
- Store Manager
- Travel Agent

The STRONG inventory has often been utilized in conjunction with the Myers–Briggs assessment. There have been many workshops where participants combine the two results to help identify skills and job preferences. Some companies also use these results for recruiting new staff. Another use of the STRONG profile is identifying reasons for job dissatisfaction. Should the respondent's answers turn out to be completely different from the job they are in, it may give them reason to rethink their job choice.

One of the better uses for the STRONG inventory is for the would-be college student. Taking the test before choosing a major may give the potential student a good idea of possible jobs that would best fit their personality and preferences. This has also been seen to be helpful for graduate students. Toni took this test in high school when she was about to transition into college, and it gave her a better idea of what sort of classes she wanted to take in college.

It's important to interpret the results correctly though, as there are some things that can skew the data. For example, women may tend to score higher in some areas that are more social in nature, simply as a result of their lack of exposure to certain areas that may traditionally be considered to be more male-oriented. According to Harmon (1994), certain career-development tests might be added to the STRONG assessment to get a more accurate picture with these groups. These tests include the Career-Development Assessment and Counseling (C-DAC), the Values Scale, and the Adult Career Concerns Inventory, to name a few.

CPP.com offers a great range of personality assessments and training in the area of personality. Their focus when describing the STRONG assessment is to point out the advantages to trainers who use it. However, this description can give you an idea of the importance of utilizing a STRONG assessment. According to CPP (2009), "The STRONG assessment offers the following benefits:

- Empowers your clients to discover their true interests so they can expand and explore various career options that will keep them engaged.
- Relates your clients' interest patterns to those of satisfied workers within an occupation.
- Presents results on a variety of complementary themes and scales.
- Delivers user-friendly, well-organized and highly intuitive results.
- When combined with the MBTI career report, provides your clients with a complete career development picture" (CPP.com, 2009).

There have been many studies showing the effectiveness of personality assessments, and the STRONG inventory is no exception. A good example of how STRONG was used involved a study done with sales agents at Mass Mutual. The training people there wanted to help their sales agents to find the areas in which they had a natural affinity to help them focus and find their path. The hope was that by understanding their strengths, the sales people could use this instrument to relieve some of their anxieties about cold calling and other such areas in sales. "For these individuals, the STRONG instrument makes the prospecting process much more real, building their confidence by showing them areas of common interest with their prospects that make their marketing efforts more focused and more effective" (CPP.com, 2009). The study proved that taking the STRONG inventory had a positive effect on their sales agents. According to the head of the Mass Mutual training department, "The most important benefit of the STRONG is that it gets people moving on the target-marketing path. It promotes action by providing another avenue for agents who are prospecting for new accounts. Further, if agents become profitable earlier, we have a better chance of retaining them and helping them build a viable, long-term financial services practice with us" (CPP.com, 2009).

Although this is a good example of how STRONG can be used with sales people, its benefits are not limited to that specific area. As Holland pointed out, people can be classified into the six different types that we mentioned previously. However, occupations can also be grouped into these same six types, where each environment may be dominated by a person who demonstrates this type of personality. "The process of self-exploration and world-of-work examination in career counseling involves matching a client's Holland type with that person's job type" (Harmon, 1994, p. 44).

"By far the most common use of the STRONG is to help people make educational and occupational choices" (Harmon, 1994, p. 3). Most people don't fit perfectly into one type, and are probably combinations of several themes. Many people may also find themselves in jobs that may not be a good match for them. "Some people are dissatisfied with their jobs because they are in positions that fail to allow them outlets for their dominant interests or because they feel they have little in common with their colleagues. Many times a profile can identify the problem by showing the individual how she or he is different" (Harmon, 1994, p. 5). You just might find that you're working next to someone who seems extremely annoyed by the job they're doing. If so, they've probably failed to take this important test to see if they're in the correct job, based on their personality. Perhaps you can drop an anonymous note on their desk with the website http://www.discoveryourpersonality.com/ Strong.html to give them a hint.

CHAPTER 11:
DISC

....

"I have to go. I'm conducting a seminar in multiple personality disorders, and it takes me forever to fill out the nametags."

— Niles Crane from Frasier (David Hyde Pierce)

Many of you may have taken what is called the DiSC profile. DiSC stands for Dominance, Influence, Submission, and Compliance. This test is quite popular in the working world, and according to the DiSC creators, "DiSC is the original, oldest, most validated, reliable, personal assessment used by over 50 million others to improve lives, interpersonal relationships, work productivity, teamwork and communication" (discprofile.com, 2009). A lawyer and psychologist named William Moulton Marston created this test. He was also responsible for creating the lie detector, or the polygraph and, strangely enough, he was also the creator of the Wonder Woman comic book.

The DiSC test was created over 35 years ago, and since then many Fortune 500 companies have used this assessment. Some of the perceived uses for the resulting information include helping with teams, training, customer service, enhancing communication, and dealing with change management.

The model has continued to evolve over the last 40 years, and like some of the other widely used tests, including Myers–Briggs, Bar-On EQ tests and others, the DiSC test has proven itself through many reliability studies, in fact the Myers–Briggs (MBTI) and the DiSC have been compared to one another for validation. As we discussed in the Myers–Briggs chapter, the MBTI was about our personal preferences, and how we prefer to take in information. The DiSC Classic test is more about surface traits, or how we behave when put into a certain environment. Therefore, where MBTI can be used to show us our behavioral strategies, the DiSC can help to increase self-awareness to help us use what we learn about ourselves, and help us in our relationships with others.

The DiSC system has also been compared to the Big Five personality prototypes, in that certain words are used to describe personality traits. In fact, of the 112 words in the DiSC profile, 27 are also in the Big Five. The creators of the DiSC state that their system differs from the Big Five in that they emphasize the positives, and try to distinguish between healthy versus unhealthy personality features.

We discussed earlier how emotional intelligence included how we dealt with stress, and the DiSC includes a component that questions how we deal with stress. The results allow you to analyze how well you deal with stress at home, at work, within personal relationships, and within your family unit.

There are several uses for the DiSC results, including, as mentioned above, team building. Respondents are able to explain their preferences in terms of how they complete tasks, and the profile deals with personal listening and what we expect out of work.

Here's a brief explanation of what the letters in 'DiSC' represent.

Dominance is about how one deals with challenges. This profile represents those who are direct and decisive. If someone has a high "D" result, they might be demanding or ambitious, and might be seen as strong-willed and challenge-seekers. These people want immediate results.

The high "D" personality can be described with a lot of "D" words, including Demanding, Determined, Driven, Dominant, Dynamic, Direct, Decisive, and Diane ... well, Diane could definitely be included here. Three percent of the population falls into this personality style, which is referred to as the Dominant Driver. They have a big ego, but can be problem solvers and risk takers, which can be a valuable addition to any team. They may come across as argumentative at times, and they don't like routine. They are also very impatient, and like to do things quickly, and because of this, they may be prone to cardiac issues. Their biggest fear is other people taking advantage of them.

The Institute for Motivational Living (2008) claims that people have different styles that they show in different environments. A high "D" personality may like to make decisions for everyone, whereas a low "D" personality may have trouble making any decision at all. When handling tasks, the high "D" wants to do things as quickly as possible; their motto is "Just do it". Unfortunately, this can come across as aggression, and may seem too forceful at times.

Some areas where a "D" could grow include doing the following things:

Learn to listen better
Give up a little control once in a while
Work on personal relationships

Explain why you want to do what you are proposing
Try to be friendlier.

Some famous examples of "D" personalities include:

Jim Kirk on Star Trek
Dirty Harry
Barbara Walters
President Nixon

Influence has to do with a person's emotional level. This pro-file represents those that are optimistic and outgoing. High "I" results may be indicative of enthusiasm and warmth. Toni definitely falls into this category. If you're on a team, you want these people, because they like to participate. They're good at sharing ideas, and have a lot of energy. These are your entertainers, who don't let the group get dull.

The high "I" personality can be described with a lot of "I" words, including Influencing, Inspiring, Independent, Inter-acting, and Interested (in people). Eleven percent of the population falls into this category, which is often called the Influencing/Inspiring style. This group of people love to talk, and are big communicators. They're probably sales or PR people, and are very friendly and sociable. Because they're so outgoing, they may end up having more extramarital affairs ... uh oh! Their biggest fear is losing social approval.

A high "I" personality may not let you get a word in edge-wise, whereas a low "I" personality may have trouble speak-ing at all. When handling tasks, the high "I" wants to do things in the most fun way possible; their motto is "You can do it". Think of the Adam Sandler movies where the guy is always yelling that out ... he's a high "I". Unfortunately, an

"I" can sometimes come across as too talkative, and can drive others crazy.

Some areas where an "I" could grow include doing the following things:

Work on being less impulsive
Control your emotions
Incorporate more facts
Listen more
Follow through.

Some famous examples of "I" personalities include:

Carol Burnett
Lucille Ball
Bill Cosby
President Reagan

Steadiness is about liking security. This profile also represents those who are sympathetic and cooperative. If someone has a low "S", they may like variety, and changing things up a bit. Generally, those in the "S" profile like to help others without necessarily getting recognized for their efforts, and they're predictable. This is the one you want to go to if you need someone to listen to your problems.

The high "S" personality can be described with a lot of "S" words, including Stable, Steady, Systematic, and Security Loving. Sixty-nine percent of the population falls into this category, which is often called the Stable Steady style. This person is easygoing and relaxed, and is probably very family-oriented. They're loyal and dependable, and therefore may stay in a bad relationship or become codependent. They probably don't like change, and can be sensitive if you criticize them. Their worst fear is that they will lose their security.

A high "S" personality doesn't like changes, whereas a low "S" personality desires change. When handling tasks, the high "S" wants to do things the easy way. Their motto is "We can do it". The downside to this type of personality is that these people can be seen as overly permissive, and even as poor performers at times.

Some areas where an "S" could grow include doing the following things:

> Embrace change
> Become more goal-oriented
> Handle confrontation
> Become more flexible
> Express your feelings.

Some famous examples of "S" personalities include:

> Mary Tyler Moore
> Mr. Rogers
> Barbara Bush
> Martin Luther King

Compliance is basically conscientiousness. This profile also represents those who are concerned and correct. High "C" people like rules and structure. They like quality, and are good planners. They prefer a system, and like to be sure that everything is accurate. This is the guy you want to hire for quality control.

The high "C" personality can be described with a lot of "C" words, including Compliant, Correct, Conservative,

Calculating, Cautious, and Conscientious. Seventeen percent of the population falls into this category, which is often called the Compliant or Correct personality. This person is very analytical, and likes facts. They may be perfectionists, and expect a high quality of work, in fact they're probably workaholics. They are very logical, probably won't be showing you their feelings very often, and like to keep the peace, so will probably not argue too much. They tend to worry a great deal, which may cause this group to have high levels of depression. Their greatest fear is that they will be criticized.

A high "C" personality may like a lot of facts and data, but a low "C" personality may get bored with all those facts and details. When handling tasks, the High "C" wants to have lots of information. They have the "Let's do it right" motto. The negative to this personality type is that they may come across as too intellectual and not talk enough.

Some areas where a "C" could grow include doing the following things:

Criticize less
Build relationships
Become decisive
Put people into the equation
Take some risks.

Some famous examples of "C" personalities include:

Spock from Star Trek
Sherlock Holmes
Meryl Streep
Albert Einstein

The DiSC has been used quite a bit because it can be helpful in the workplace to get people to work together at all levels. By understanding our behavior, as well as that of others, we can learn adaptation techniques. This should improve communications, and allow diversity to be more easily understood. This, in turn, should improve team performance and reduce the amount of group conflict.

Just as the Myers–Briggs MBTI test showed introverted and extroverted parts to one's personality, so does the DiSC. Those with a high "C" or "S" style tend to fall into the introverted or passive side, while those with a high "D" or "I" style tend to fall into the outgoing/extroverted or outspoken side. Those who are "D"s and "C"s tend to be more task-oriented, while "I"s and "S"s tend to be more people-oriented.

As with many personality tests, in order to discover which type you are, you must choose words that you feel most and least describe you. What's interesting about this assessment is that the results are placed into three different graphs. The first graph gives you information about your public self, the second about your private self, and the third about your perceived self. Huh? Why are there three "you's"? According to the DiSC method, you have a mask, or public self, of how others see you, which gives you the information for the first graph. You also have an instinctive self that was influenced at a very young age, and that is your core or private self, which gives you the information for the second graph. Lastly there is the way you see yourself, which is your mirror, or self-identity. This gives you the information for the third and final graph.

So, if there are three graphs, which one do you look at? Technically, you can look at all three of them to get different perspectives, however the third one tends to be the one that people use to find your highest personality type. What is different about this test versus the Myers–Briggs test, for example, is that these results can change over time. Further, when we look at this test versus something like the MBTI, we see that people are combinations of types, and not just strictly one type. Therefore, your highest letter may be a "C", but your second highest letter may be a "D", which would make you a "C/D" personality. This is Diane's type.

There are a lot of good things about this assessment for the business environment. Since teams do better with diverse members, it's important to have an understanding of what each member of the team brings to the table. It's also important to know how to get along with your fellow team members, who are of a different type to you. If everyone on a team was a "D", there would be a lot of head-butting going on, and not a lot of smooth sailing. It's important for leaders to choose team that contain different types of personalities so that everyone's weaknesses can be compensated for by the opposing personality.

The Institute for Motivational Living (2008) claims there are four things you can do once you know what your style is. You can modify it, capitalize on it, augment it, or blend it. If you're going to modify your personality, you'll need to work on areas where you can grow, but this requires you to choose change, repeat that change, and follow through. If you're going to capitalize on your style, you need to identify your strengths and promote them. Augmenting one's style is often done in the team environment, where one person's style offsets another's weaker style. Lastly, if you're going to blend your style, you may need to make some short-term changes in your personality to accommodate other people's needs.

CHAPTER 12:
STRENGTHS FINDER

....

*"If it weren't for caffeine I'd have
no personality whatsoever!"*

— Anonymous

In a college foresight course Diane teaches, she utilizes a book by Tom Rath titled *Strengths Finder*. In this book, the author discusses how you can figure out your top five talents so that you can do that job that you were meant to do. He claims that too many people are not tapping into their natural talents. Over 40 years of research has gone into this system, according to which there are 34 talents that we all could have. By taking the assessment, you can figure out where your strengths lie. According to Rath, "People have several times more potential for growth when they invest energy in developing their strengths instead of correcting their deficiencies." In other words, it's easier to not swim upstream! We should go with the flow of our talents. Rath claims that, "Our studies indicate that people who do have the opportunity to focus on their strengths every day are six times as likely to be engaged in their jobs and more than three times as likely to report having an excellent quality of life in general."

How do we follow this path of least resistance? The first thing to do is figure out your strengths. Instead of telling yourself you can do anything, you might be better off doing the things that you are really good at doing. It is more about being more of what you are in the first place, instead of trying to create something out of nothing. The name of the assessment, *Strengths Finder*, may be misleading, because it's actually more about your talents than your actual strengths. To get to the strength, you actually have to take your talent and invest time developing it. In other words, talent multiplied by investment will give you your strengths.

Based upon the results from this test, there are 34 talents:

Achiever: This is about your drive and need for achievement. Are you driven to succeed? Can you work long hours and enjoy it? If so, you're probably a high achiever.

Activator: How anxious are you to start things? This is about how your actions lead to actual performance. You're quick to make decisions and look for results. You need to get things done.

Adaptability: You live in the here and now. You may have plans, but you're all about today. You have no problem with things coming up to disrupt your day, because you're very flexible.

Analytical: Do you require proof? If so, you're analytical. You're that little kid that never stops saying "why?" You're interested in cause and effect, logical, and don't like wishful thinking.

Arranger: Arrangers like to conduct and juggle things. They're flexible, and don't mind when the unexpected shows up. They like figuring things out and looking for new ways to do things.

Belief: This theme is about values. For you to have happiness in your life, you require belief. This gives you direction, and allows you to trust. You'll need to be in a job that you find meaningful.

Command: This is the take-charge person. Your opinion is very important to you, so you tend to share it a lot. You don't mind confrontation, and you may be a risk-taker. Your presence draws people to you.

Communication: You're a natural speaker or storyteller. You want what you say to have great meaning. People are drawn to hear you speak. You may inspire others to act based upon your words.

Competition: You're very aware of what everyone else is doing, and how you compare with them. You're all about contests and winning. It's not all about playing the game, but who wins that matters. If you don't think you can win, you probably won't play.

Connectedness: You enjoy the thought that we all have a collective unconscious. You feel that we're all tied together somehow. This gives you comfort that you like to share with others.

Consistency: You're all about balance, and don't like favoritism. You like a consistent atmosphere to work in where you know what to expect. You want predictability.

Context: You need to look behind you to understand what is ahead of you. You want to know why people came to be the way they are. Perhaps that's why you're reading this book. You're a big fan of blueprints.

Deliberative: You may be seen as very careful due to the fact that you see the world as unpredictable. You like to identify risks. You may be waiting for the other shoe to drop all of the time.

Developer: Do you see potential in others? Then you may be a developer. You like helping others succeed. You like to see growth. People will seek you out for your encouragement and helpfulness.

Discipline: You prefer predictability. Everything is about planning and routines. You're great with deadlines. This makes you a controlling person. You try to help others understand your need for this control. You're not someone who would like to have a surprise party.

Empathy: You're able to feel what others are feeling, see what they are seeing, and share a common perspective. Empathy, not to be confused with sympathy, means you don't feel pity, just an understanding.

Focus: You like knowing where you're going, and you get frustrated when you don't. This makes you filter out things so that you head in the right direction. You don't do well with delays. If you're on a team, you tend to bring others back into focus, making you a valuable team member.

Futuristic: You love to think about the future. It inspires and energizes you. You have the ability to explain that future to others in a vivid picture. You inspire hope in those around you.

Harmony: You want everyone to get along. You don't do well with conflict, or with people who waste their time with it. You tend not to give your opinions, in order to keep the peace. You don't want to rock the boat.

Ideation: Ideas are fascinating to you. You love new discoveries, in fact you get a boost of energy just from having a new idea pop into your head. You're creative, and probably intelligent.

Includer: You don't like leaving anybody out. If you're on a team at work, you'll welcome the new guy. You're very accepting of others' personalities. Everyone is equal in your eyes.

Individualization: You like to see the differences in people. You're probably a people watcher. You tend to be the person to go out of your way to get the exact birthday gift for someone in order to fit their personality. You can see how each individual on the team can bring something of importance to the table.

Input: You like to collect things, because you find a lot of different things interesting. You might be a bit of a pack rat because you see so many potential uses for things.

Intellection: You're a thinker. You require mental activity, and are introspective. You might drive yourself a bit crazy over-thinking some situations. You may also be a loner, because you enjoy being alone with your thoughts.

Learner: You enjoy the process of learning even more than the end result of what you have learned. Facts thrill you. You love to take on new subject matter.

Maximizer: You're not happy with being average, and want to be your best. You're all about excellence, and are attracted to others who feel the same way. If someone tries to change you, you're repelled by them.

Positivity: You tend to give a lot of praise, are enthusiastic, and have a lot of energy. You may come across as dramatic. If someone criticizes you, it doesn't bring you down.

Relator: You like relationships and meeting new and different people. Intimacy doesn't frighten you. You like to understand others' aspirations, fears, and feelings. You don't mind taking a risk in order to have that close relationship.

Responsibility: You like commitment. You feel horrible if you disappoint someone else. You're obsessed with doing the right thing. You get things done, so you may be the go-to guy in the group. You like to volunteer.

Restorative: You're a problem solver. You see problems as challenges, and enjoy finding solutions. You like to restore what is old to new. You're a fixer, and keep things from dying.

Self-Assurance: You have self-confidence, which comes from a deep faith in yourself. Risks are OK if you know you can deliver. You trust your own judgment. No one is able to tell you what you should be thinking.

Significance: You like recognition. You want others to hear you, and you like being known. You'd like to be seen in a positive light as credible and successful. You're independent, with lots of goals.

Strategic: You see patterns that enable you to make it through confusion. You evaluate possible roadblocks to figure out the right path. You're always looking at the "what if" scenario.

Woo: You like meeting new people. Strangers may give you a sense of energy that draws you to them. You initiate conversations, and enjoy making the connections. You're a schmoozer.

Now that you have an idea of these strengths, you may be curious as to how we turned out. Diane had the following results:

Achiever
Competition
Learner
Individualization
Activator

Therefore based on these results, Diane is a hard worker with a strong work ethic. She is also very competitive, and likes to win. She always likes learning new things. She enjoys seeing all of the differences in people. Lastly, she makes things happen. What does all of that tell you? Well, if you take the test, you're given a report that gives you job suggestions based upon these personality traits. By doing those jobs where you have natural abilities, you'll be working within your abilities, rather than trying to swim upstream. Once you take the test and have your results, there's a file you can print out that suggests things that will work better for you in the workplace. What it doesn't do is tell you the exact job you should have. It just gives you guidelines for the things you should look for within your employment so that you're in an environment where you can best utilize your skills. The point of taking such a test is to uncover talents that you may not have realized you had, and to make you realize the futility in trying to create talents you don't have already.

CHAPTER 13:
OTHER PERSONALITY ASSESSMENTS

"My one regret in life is that I am not someone else."

— Woody Allen

We have covered some of what we feel are the most useful and popular tests out there, however there are quite a few others on the market that are also utilized by companies and individuals. Some of these are better thought of or more reliable than others. We'll discuss a few of them here, just to give you an idea of how you might utilize their information. We thought we'd begin with some of the very early assessments, to give you an idea of where the whole concept of personality testing may have gotten started.

THE FOUR TEMPERAMENTS OR FOUR HUMOURS

No book on personality tests would be complete without mentioning one of the first areas of personality assessments developed by the Greeks, Hippocrates and Plato. "In Greek medicine around 2500 years ago it was believed that in order to maintain health, people needed an even balance of the four body fluids: blood, phlegm, yellow bile and black bile. These four body fluids were linked (in daft ways by modern standards) to certain organs and illnesses and also represented the Four Temperaments or Four Humours (of personality) as they later became known"(Businessballs.

com, 2009). The Greeks were concerned with maintaining a balance between these areas to ward off illnesses.

Without getting into too much detail, these four areas of blood, phlegm, and yellow and black bile were interpreted by Hippocrates into Four Humours, which he translated to cheerful, somber, enthusiastic, and calm. Later, a guy named Galen saw these four personality characteristics as sanguine, melancholic, choleric, and phlegmatic. Wait ... what's that? Okay, jump ahead in time, and if you've already forgotten, go back to Chapter 2 and Myers–Briggs, and you'll see that these four areas have been changed to SP (sensing and perceiving), SJ (sensing and judging), NF (intuitive and feeling), and lastly NT (intuitive and thinking). Keirsey later took the Myers–Briggs definitions and came up with the Artisan, the Rationalist, the Guardian, and the Idealist. No matter what researchers have called the four types of personality, one thing they all seem to agree upon is that people are not solely one thing or another; they all have a little bit of all of these things, although some of us have more of some parts than others ... makes sense!

THE WONDERLIC TEST

In the 1930s, a guy named Eldon F. Wonderlic developed the Wonderlic Personality Test (WPT) based on cognitive abilities. His assessment became more popular during World War II, as it was used to select candidates to become pilots. Later, his son, Chuck, expanded the use of this assessment. If you've heard of it, that's probably due to its popularity in the world of football. "One of the most enthusiastic users was Tom Landry of the Dallas Cowboys. Coach Landry found that the WPT scores were related to learning the team playbook and to adaptability" (Wonderlic.com, 2009).

A person with average intelligence should get a score of around 20 when they take the test. This would indicate an IQ of about 100. Paul Zimmerman wrote *The New Thinking Man's Guide to Pro Football* in 1984, and for all you sports lovers out there, the material contained in this book might be an easy way to understand these test scores. In his book, Zimmerman listed the average scores for football players. These include:

Offensive tackle – 26
Center – 25
Quarterback – 24
Guard – 23
Tight end – 22
Safety – 19
Linebacker – 19
Cornerback – 18
Wide Receiver – 17
Fullback – 17
Halfback – 16

"While an average football player usually scores around 20 points, Wonderlic Inc. claims that a score of at least 10 points suggests a person is literate. Furthermore, when the test was given to miscellaneous people from various professions, it was observed that the average participant scored a 24. Examples of scores from everyday professions included:

Chemist – 31
Programmer – 29
Journalist – 26
Sales – 24
Bank teller – 22
Clerical worker – 21
Security guard – 17
Warehouse – 15" (Wikipedia)

This test is used in many other areas outside of sports, in fact the Wonderlic site lists many results from their clients, who come from a vast array of industries. "The WPT-R employment test takes only 12 minutes to complete. It is administered online or via a pencil and paper faxed answer sheet and automatically scored by Wonderlic. The WPT-R helps measure a candidate's ability to:

- Learn a specific job
- Solve problems
- Understand instructions
- Apply knowledge to new situations
- Benefit from specific job training
- Be satisfied with a particular job.

Using the WPT-R in your employee selection process helps you to match people with positions that suit their learning speed and aptitude" (Wonderlic.com, 2009).

THE BIRKMAN METHOD

In the 1940s, a man named Roger W. Birkman created a personality testing instrument called the Birkman Method®, which was about studying social comprehension. "The Birkman Method® accurately measures productive behaviors, underlying needs and motivations, stress behaviors and organizational orientation. Application of The Birkman Method® enables higher levels of performance for individuals, teams and organizations and reduces stress behaviors" (Birkman.com, 2009). "In brief, The Birkman Method® includes the following five major perspectives:

- **Usual Behavior** – an individual's effective behavioral style of dealing with relationships and tasks.

- **Underlying Needs** – an individual's expectations of how relationships and social situations should be governed in the context of the relationship or situation.
- **Stress Behaviors** – an individual's ineffective style of dealing with relationships or tasks; behavior observed when underlying needs are not met.
- **Interests** – an individual's expressed preference for job titles based on the assumption of equal economic rewards.
- **Organizational Focus** – the perspective in which an individual views problems and solutions relating to organizational goals" (Birkman.com, 2009).

One of the goals of taking the Birkman Method test is to find where your interest lies. The areas of interest include such things as social service, persuasive, outdoor, literary, clerical, numerical, artistic, mechanical, scientific, and musical. The results of the assessment give your interests in a ranked order. For example, you might be strongest in clerical, followed by artistic, then musical, etc. As we mentioned earlier the Myers–Briggs test gave an indication of preferences. This test has the added value of including motivational factors, and discusses things that affect one's expectations or behaviors.

THE PERSONALITY SELF-PORTRAIT

Dr. John Oldham and Lois Morris wrote a book about assessing your personality titled the *Personality Self-Portrait*. What makes this appraisal different is that it's useful in diagnosing personality disorders, as well as explaining your personality in general. The authors explain how to utilize this information about your personality, and how it affects your relationships, work, self-image, emotions, self-control, and spirituality. They explain that personality is genetically influenced, but that you can grow and develop throughout your life, unless you have a personality disorder, which may be more difficult to change.

This assessment assigns people to one of fourteen personality self-portraits. That also means there is the possibility of having one of fourteen personality disorders should your version of those self-portraits be an over-exaggeration of that profile. The instrument that is used to measure your personality consists of 107 questions, the answers to which offer insight into your personality. We probably sound like a broken record, but just like the other assessments, no one is really one type or one style; we're all a combination of personality traits. And again, you'll likely find that you're higher in some areas than in others. It's an interesting assessment to take, as it shows you your most dominant styles. The fourteen styles, based on this assessment, are:

1. **Conscientious Style:** This style includes things such as being a hard worker, being a perfectionist, and sometimes being a bit of a collector or a pack rat. This was Diane's highest area. This person is very self-disciplined. They do well with a person who has a dramatic personality. If you work with someone like this, you have to let them do their thing, and not assume you have to keep up with them. They like to win, so you probably won't win any arguments. When you hear someone referred to as type A, that's this person to the max. The disorder side of this personality type includes being obsessive-compulsive. They may become so conscientious that they over do it and can't possibly keep up with reality. This can lead to high stress!

2. **Self-Confident Style:** This is your basic leader. This guy thinks highly of himself, is very competitive, and has great poise and stature. He knows he can do whatever it is he needs to do. If you work with him, be sure you're loyal and don't need a lot of directions, because they assume you know how to do your job. Two self-confident types could be a good love match, but they may want to watch out for each other's temper, because they'll both have one. The disorder side of this personality type includes being narcissistic. They may get to the point of thinking too highly of themselves, may become manipulative, and may lack empathy.

3. **Devoted Style:** This is the caring person who is committed, a great follower on a team, into harmony, and very considerate. They will sacrifice to get things done, which makes them a good worker. A conscientious person may be a good match for them. The disorder side of this personality type includes being too dependent. They may try too hard to please others and have a tough time with decisions.

4. **Dramatic Style:** We all know the fun, flamboyant guy in the office. They're usually very well groomed, like a lot of attention, and can be very engaging. This person can come across as emotional, and may seem to wear their heart on their sleeve. They like excitement, which can lead to stormy relationships. They match well with a conscientious type, but if two dramatics get together, there may be conflict. Be sure to give your dramatic co-worker lots of compliments, because they're looking for them. The disorder side of this personality type includes being histrionic. This

means they may have an obsessive need to be the center of attention, and may push the envelope in order to get it. This may lead to inappropriate behavior, such as sexual harassment, etc.

5. **Vigilant Style:** The authors refer to this guy as the survivor. They're very aware of everything around them. They can be autonomous, and cautious, but very loyal. This person needs to control, so doesn't do real well with an aggressive personality. They'd be better matched with a conscientious type. The disorder side of this personality type includes becoming paranoid. This may lead them to not want to confide in others, and to hold grudges.

6. **Sensitive Style:** This is the person who would rather stay home and avoid socializing. They like the familiar, and may seem somewhat restrained, as they keep to themselves. They're very private people, and tend to worry a lot. They do well around self-confident or dramatic types. If you work with them, avoid forcing them to do things that make them uncomfortable. You may have to compromise to make them more willing to do certain more adventurous things, such as traveling or dealing with the unfamiliar. The disorder side of this personality type includes becoming avoidant, i.e. they may get to the point of avoiding people. This may also cause great inhibitions, and an inferiority complex.

7. **Leisurely Style:** This is the easy-going guy. They want to stop and smell the roses. They feel like they can put it off until tomorrow if need be. They like to be around others, and can be very family-oriented. They would

do well with a Devoted person, or one who is Self-Sacrificing. The guy who wrote "Don't Worry, Be Happy" is probably this type. The disorder side of this personality type includes becoming passive-aggressive. They may feel misunderstood, and become sullen or possibly hostile because of it.

8. **Adventurous Style:** This guy likes a challenge. Society's norms are of no interest to them. They may want to sew some wild oats with no regrets. They like action, and are out for themselves. They aren't a fan of "the system". While they may do well in a relationship with another adventurous person, they probably aren't looking for a long-term relationship, because this would require too much sacrifice. The disorder side of this personality type includes becoming antisocial. Their failure to conform may leader to illegal behaviors. They may become too impulsive and reckless.

9. **Idiosyncratic Style:** This isn't your conventional guy. They may have their own belief systems, and seem to live in their own world. This guy is drawn to metaphysics, and likes to observe others. They're so open-minded that they may come across as a bit off. Since they can be on their own, they may remain single. The disorder side of this personality type includes becoming schizotypal. This means they may get into really odd things like magical thinking, become paranoid, and become excessively anxious in social encounters.

10. **Solitary Style:** We all know the loner personality. They like their solitude and independence. Since their

emotions are self-contained, they come across as stoic. They do best with a conscientious partner. Although they may seem uncomfortable, they may be just fine; it's just part of how they come across. Leave them alone, and don't keep asking them what's wrong. The disorder side of this personality type includes developing a schizoid personality. This means they won't be able to get really close to anyone, may find things aren't pleasurable, and may become emotionally cold.

11. **Mercurial Style:** If you like roller coasters, you'll like this guy. It's all ups and downs. They're very intense, uninhibited, and open-minded. This may lead to relationship problems though, because they require a lot of intensity. They may be attracted to those who are also mercurial types, but the fire may not last. Try to tolerate their moods at work, and realize they may be impulsive. The disorder side of this personality type includes developing a borderline personality. With impulsivity may come recklessness, instability, and suicidal behavior.

12. **Self-Sacrificing Style:** This is the giver. They're very generous, and like to help others. They're also very considerate and non-judgmental. They probably don't want to get attention for their good deeds though. They can be a good match for just about any other personality type. At work, remember, even if they say they don't want attention, they do appreciate being complimented. Try to avoid taking advantage of their good nature. The disorder side of this personality type includes developing self-defeating behaviors. They may turn down things

that could be pleasurable, or avoid those who treat them well, as a way of filling an overly self-sacrificing need.

13. **Aggressive Style:** This guy wants to be the boss. They like command and taking control. They're brave and adventurous, and like to be at the front of the line. They do well with Devoted, Sensitive, or Self-Sacrificing partners. At work, be careful not to go around this person, because they'll resent it. They like to win, so be prepared if they lose. They're all about reason and not feelings, and may have a nasty temper if you push them. The disorder side of this personality type may lead to sadism. They may start to enjoy physical cruelty, humiliating others, or even inflicting pain.

14. **Serious Style:** This person is very realistic. There are no pretenses and no surprises here. They're hard working, and probably not the life of the party. The good thing is, they're realistic about relationships, and allow imperfections. The disorder side of this personality type includes developing a depressive personality. They may become overly moody, critical, and brooding. Pessimism may get the best of them, as well as guilt.

THE KOLBE INDEX

The Kolbe Index is a series of tests created by educator Kathy Kolbe that focus on three areas: Thinking, Feeling, and Doing. According to Kolbe, her tests can help you leverage your talents to find the perfect career. Her premise is that you may be wasting your talents in a job that does not fit your personality, and her tests can be taken at www. kolbe.com for a fee.

"The Kolbe A index is a forced-choice instrument which requires subjects to choose one of four responses reflecting how they would be most and least likely to respond to 36 single-sentence problem-solving or behavioral scenarios. It is part of the Kolbe RightFit™ System, based on the theory of conation, which premises human behavior on the inter-action between the cognitive (knowledge), the affective (feeling or belief), and the conative (instinct or will). The Kolbe A index raw scores are translated into a set of four scales which reflect the subject's conative instincts" (ware-withal.com, 2009).

THE CAREER KEY

Remember our buddy John Holland? Well, a guy named Dr. Lawrence Jones created an assessment called the Career Key based upon measuring Holland's six personality types. This Career Key, or CK as he calls it, is supposed to give you insight into your best career matches based upon your per-sonality. To find out more about this, check out http://www. careerkey.org/.

MAPP

In line with finding that perfect job, you might want to take the Motivational Appraisal of Personal Potential test, or MAPP. This test is more about your temperament, and how your aptitudes for certain things influence your career choices. To take this test, check out http://www.assess-ment.com/. The creators of this test claim that over 6 million people have taken it. What's cool about this one is that it's offered in the following languages: Arabic, Bulgarian,

Chinese, English, French, Kings English, Korean, Polish, Portuguese, Russian, Romanian, Slovakian, Spanish, and Swedish. We thought about trying to get Toni's sister Terra to take it in Spanish and Portuguese, as well as English, since she speaks all of those languages. We wanted to see if the results were any different if she answered in another language. Hmm ... we may still have to try that.

CAREER TESTS

If the end result is to get a job based on taking a personality assessment, you shouldn't overlook Monster and other such sites. Monster has a "Discover Your Perfect Career Quiz", which bases its results on your personality type. Check out www.Monster.com for more information on that. What's good about their test is that they help you narrow down your field of job possibilities.

IQ

Many people ask whether IQ tests fit into this mix of understanding personality, but IQ is not really about personality. IQ stands for Intelligence Quotient, and it's more about intelligence than personality. Like EQ, which as you'll recall stands for Emotional Quotient, it can be developed or improved. In fact, since the early 20th century, IQ scores have gone up several points on average every decade. They refer to this phenomenon as the Flynn effect, named after a guy named James R. Flynn, who liked to talk about it a lot, but the real point was actually made by the authors of *The Bell Curve*. They claimed that, "Intelligence is a better predictor of many factors including financial income, job performance, unwed pregnancy, and crime than parents' socioeconomic status or education level."

To get an idea of what your IQ score means, check out this chart:

IQ Range	Intelligence Classification
25 – 40	Severe mental disability
40 – 55	Moderate mental disability
55 – 70	Mild mental disability
70 – 85	Borderline mental disability
85 – 115	Average
115 – 130	Above average
130 – 145	Moderately gifted
145 – 160	Highly gifted
160 – 175	Exceptionally gifted
Over 175	Profoundly gifted

ASTROLOGY AND PERSONALITY

Many people think that one's astrological sign has something to do with one's personality. If this were true, then all Libras would be alike, just as all Scorpios would be similar, etc. Although the science behind personality traits and astrology is not exactly there, it might be fun to see what the astrologers of the world say your personality should be like based upon your sign.

Your astrological or zodiac sign is determined by how the planets were aligned when you were born. Astrologists claim that this order has an effect on this world, which can affect your personality. According to Helium.com, each of the signs has various strengths and weaknesses associated with it.

- **Capricorn** – December 22nd – January 19th
  Strengths: Practicality, ambitious, disciplined, humorous, patient, loyal
  Weaknesses: Miserly, unimaginative, conceited, distrusting
- **Aquarius** – January 20th – February 18th
  Strengths: Friendly, loyal, honest, inventive, independent, intellectual
  Weaknesses: Stubborn, sarcastic, aloof, unemotional, unattached
- **Pisces** – February 19th – March 20th
  Strengths: Compassionate, devoted, imaginative, adaptable, intuitive
  Weaknesses: Secretive, vague, self-pitying, lazy, indecisive, oversensitive
- **Aries** – March 21st – April 19th
  Strengths: Independent, generous, enthusiastic, optimistic, quick-witted, courageous
  Weaknesses: Selfish, impulsive, impatient, quick-tempered, moody
- **Taurus** – April 20th – May 20th
  Strengths: Loving, patient, determined, reliable, persistent, loyal
  Weaknesses: Self-indulgent, materialistic, stubborn, jealous, possessive
- **Gemini** – May 21st – June 21st
  Strengths: Energetic, adaptable, clever, imaginative, intellectual, lively

....

Weaknesses: Tense, superficial, cunning, devious, restless

- **Cancer** – June 22nd – July 22nd
  Strengths: Emotional, loving, protective, sympathetic, intuitive, caring, loyal
  Weaknesses: Clingy, oversensitive, self-absorbed, emotional, moody
- **Leo** – July 23rd – August 22nd
  Strengths: Confident, loyal, ambitious, generous, creative, enthusiastic
  Weaknesses: Bossy, interfering, intolerant, patronizing, vain, melodramatic
- **Virgo** – August 23rd – September 22nd
  Strengths: Observant, reliable, helpful, analytical, modest, practical
  Weaknesses: Over-critical, conservative, perfectionist, skeptical, interfering
- **Libra** – September 23rd – October 23rd
  Strengths: Diplomatic, peaceful, intuitive, idealistic, charming, sociable
  Weaknesses: easily influenced, flirtatious, self-indulgent, unreliable
- **Scorpio** – October 24th – November 22nd
  Strengths: Passionate, dynamic, local, determined, exciting, intuitive
  Weaknesses: Compulsive, obsessive, jealous, secretive, manipulative
- **Sagittarius** – November 23rd – December 22nd
  Strengths: Good-humored, honest, intellectual, independent, optimistic
  Weaknesses: Irresponsible, restless, tactless, unemotional, careless

Although it may be a lot of fun to look at your astrological sign in the morning paper, you may not want to put a lot of faith in what these forecasts tell you. A common joke is, Will astrology become a legitimate science? My horoscope told me so. What's interesting is that there are actually certified and counterfeit astrologers. According to elbertwade.com, a certified astrologer is "One who has studied long, read widely, completed structured astrological courses at various levels, practiced – as part of the learning process (usually without being paid) – and then received a professional certification from a *recognized* astrological organization or reputable school – but only after completing an intensive (usually day-long, closely and professionally monitored) examination equivalent to a 'board exam' for various other professions." They defined a counterfeit astrologer as including "all those who are just everyday, run-of-the-mill, out-and-out fortunetellers who only try to use Astrology to dress up their acts mainly because fewer people are likely to pay much to see just a plain-vanilla 'fortune-teller,' but many more may think these persons could be more legitimate because they use such scientific catch-words as 'Astrology,' 'horoscopes,' and 'astrologer' in all their ads, on their carnival/sideshow tents, and those gaudy roadside billboards" (elbertwade.com, 2009).

One of the many problems with astrology is that it assumes that our universe is finite. Although it may be amusing to look at horoscopes, chances are they probably don't tell you a lot about your true personality. If you've ever met anyone with exactly the same birthday as yours, you probably found that you weren't exactly alike.

ADDITIONAL TESTS AND SITES

The following is hardly an exhaustive list, but it's at least a starting point for some of the online personality tests you can take:

http://www.businessballs.com/tests.htm
http://www.keirsey.com/kts.html
http://www.humanmetrics.com/cgi-win/JTypes1.htm
http://www.ideodynamic.com/enneagram-monthly/index.htm
http://www.mirrorgate.com/
http://www.personalitypage.com/home.html
http://www.haleonline.com/psych
http://www.2h.com/personality-tests.html
http://ivillage.advisorteam.com/
http://www.personalitytypepage.com/info.html
http://www.win.net/insightsys/question.htm
http://www.psychtests.com/
http://www.socionics.com/sta/sta-1-r.html
http://www.queendom.com
HelpSelf.com
http://www.outofservice.com/bigfive/
http://directory.google.com/Top/Science/Social_Sciences/Psychology/Personality/Tests/

Lastly, a very influential, credible, and valid test that many people may overlook when taking personality assessments can be found at http://www.matthewbarr.co.uk/trek/. This is the Star Trek Personality Test. Diane was very happy to find out she came out as Commander Data, until she read the notation under his profile that stated, "I am incapable of any feeling." Wow, that's harsh! But then again, she did score a zero on the F for feeling part of the Myers–Briggs assessment.

CHAPTER 14:
PERSONALITY DISORDERS

"A narcissist is someone better looking than you are."

— Gore Vidal

So far, we've addressed personality in terms of those traits or qualities whereby a person would be considered normal, but no book on personality would be complete without some discussion of personality disorders, which we touched on briefly in Chapter 11. Halcyon.com describes a personality disorder as, "An enduring pattern of inner experience and behavior that deviates markedly from the expectation of the individual's culture, is pervasive and inflexible, has an onset in adolescence or early adulthood, is stable over time, and leads to distress or impairment" (2009). One of the most commonly heard of personality disorders is narcissism. You may think of narcissism as being egotistical, or having a big ego. Freud believed that, "Some narcissism is an essential part of all of us from birth." According to Freud, there was such as a thing as healthy narcissistic qualities. However, having high levels of narcissistic traits can become a personality disorder.

Hotchkiss (2003) lists what she describes as The Seven Deadly Sins of Narcissism.

1. Shamelessness
2. Magical thinking
3. Arrogance
4. Envy
5. Entitlement
6. Exploitation
7. Bad Boundaries

Hollywood and the world of literature has shown us some narcissistic personalities. Oscar Wilde wrote *The Picture of Dorian Gray* about a man who didn't age in real life, while a painting of him that he kept locked away did. Anyone who's a fan of Christian Bale has probably seen his portrayal of a scary narcissist in *American Psycho*. There's usually something about these characters that shows their grandiosity or, in layman's terms, their self-importance.

A narcissist lacks empathy. As you may recall, having empathy was a big part of being emotionally intelligent. The narcissist looks at everything from the point of view of how it will affect them personally. They're unable to step into your shoes and feel what you feel.

Halcyon (2009) describes narcissists as having the following qualities.

1. An exaggerated sense of self-importance.
2. Preoccupation with fantasies of unlimited success, power, brilliance, beauty, or ideal love.
3. Believes he is special and can only be understood by, or should associate with, other special or high-status people (or institutions).
4. Requires excessive admiration.
5. Has a sense of entitlement.

6. Selfishly takes advantage of others to achieve his own ends.
7. Lacks empathy.
8. Is often envious of others or believes that others are envious of him.
9. Shows arrogant, haughty, patronizing, or contemptuous behaviors or attitudes.

Narcissists are often the source of material for jokes:

"How many narcissists does it take to change a light bulb? (a) Just one – but he has to wait for the whole world to revolve around him; (b) None at all – he hires menials for work that's beneath him" (Halcyon.com).

Although narcissists may be hard on other people, criticizing their every move, they don't like to receive criticism, in fact any criticism of them could evoke a hostile reaction. Perhaps because they see themselves in such a brilliant light, it can be hard for them to understand why anyone would see them any other way. "As Freud said of narcissists, these people act like they're in love with themselves. And they are in love with an ideal image of themselves—or they want you to be in love with their pretend self, it's hard to tell just what's going on" (Halcyon.com). Because they think they're perfect, they can't see that they have a personality disorder.

You may have seen a television show featuring Dr. Drew Pinsky called *Celebrity Rehab with Dr. Drew*. He's had a lot of interaction with celebrities who are notoriously narcissistic, and wrote a book with S. Mark Young called *The Mirror Effect: How Celebrity Narcissism is Seducing America*. In the book, there's a 40-question Narcissistic Personality Inventory. To see an online copy of this test, check out http://www.

usatoday.com/news/health/2009-03-16-pinsky-quiz_N.htm. The authors claim that, "The average score for the general population is 15.3. The average score for celebrities is 17.8. Pinsky says he scored 16" (USAtoday.com, 2009).

If you recall, we mentioned a psychiatrist called Karen Horney earlier in the book. She developed a personality theory called the NPA personality test, which is based upon genetic traits. In her work, she identified some personality behavioral traits that included Narcissism, Perfectionism, and Aggression.

Some people suggest that things such as Facebook and Twitter add to the narcissistic personality's self-importance issues. HolyMoly.com (2009) recently posted its top-40 list of celebrities who love themselves the most based on their Twitter use:

1. Russell Brand

2. Katy Perry

3. Lily Allen

4. Ashton Kutcher

5. Chris Moyles

6. Fred Durst

7. Demi Moore

8. Holly Willoughby

9. Fearne Cotton

10. Jamie Oliver

11. P Diddy

12. Perez Hilton

13. Andi Peters

14. Ryan Seacrest

15. Eddie Izzard

16. Charlie Brooker

17. Graham Norton

18. Paul Daniels

19. Richard Bacon

20. Matthew Horne

21. Solange Knowles

22. Matt Lucas

23. Alex Zane

24. Calvin Harris

25. Katie Price

26. Justin Lee Collins

27. Graham Coxon

28. Coldplay

29. Greg Wallace

30. Phillip Schofield

31. Peter Andre

32. Billie Piper

33. Adam Woodyatt

34. Jonathan Ross

35. Phil Jupitus

36. Jimmy Carr

37. Mike Skinner

38. Richard Branson

39. Britney Spears

40. Stephen Fry

MentalHelp.net (2009) recently included some interesting statistics about narcissists.

- Most narcissists (75%) are men.
- NPD (Narcissistic Personality Disorder) is one of a "family" of personality disorders (formerly known as Cluster B). Other members: Borderline PD, Antisocial PD and Histrionic PD.

- NPD is often diagnosed with other mental health disorders (co-morbidity) – or with substance abuse, or impulsive and reckless behaviors (dual diagnosis).
- NPD is a new (1980) mental health category in the Diagnostic and Statistics Manual (DSM).
- There is only scant research regarding narcissism. But what there is has not demonstrated any ethnic, social, cultural, economic, genetic, or professional predilection to NPD.
- It is estimated that 0.7–1% of the general population suffer from NPD.
- Pathological narcissism was first described in detail by Freud. Other major contributors are Klein, Horney, Kohut, Kernberg, Millon, Roningstam, Gunderson, and Hare.
- The onset of narcissism is in infancy, childhood, and early adolescence. It is commonly attributed to childhood abuse and trauma inflicted by parents, authority figures, or even peers.
- There is a whole range of narcissistic reactions – from the mild, reactive, and transient to the permanent personality disorder.
- Narcissists are either "Cerebral" (derive their narcissistic supply from their intelligence or academic achievements) or "Somatic" (derive their narcissistic supply from their physique, exercise, physical or sexual prowess, and "conquests").
- Narcissists are either "Classic" – see definition below – or they are "Compensatory", or "Inverted" – see definitions here: "The Inverted Narcissist" – http://www.geocities.com/vaksam/faq66.html.
- NPD is treated in talk therapy (psychodynamic or cognitive-behavioral). The prognosis for an adult narcissist is poor, though his adaptation to life and

to others can improve with treatment. Medication is applied to side-effects and behaviors (such as mood or affect disorders and obsession-compulsion) – usually with some success."

As we mentioned above, part of being narcissistic is having a sense of entitlement. In Twenge and Campbell's (2009) book *The Narcissism Epidemic*, the authors discuss what they call "Generation Me". Are younger generations becoming more narcissistic? "Self-esteem is at an all-time high in most groups, with more than 80% of recent college students scoring higher in general self-esteem than the average 1960s college student" (Twenge and Campbell, 2009, p. 13). The authors claim that as a nation we have slowly changed our focus to self-admiration. Kids are told they are special. Could it all come back to Freud's pleasure principle that states, "People seek pleasure and avoid pain?"

The problem with self-importance and entitlement in the business world "often boils down to an equation: Less work for more pay" (Twenge and Campbell, 2009, p. 235). So, we're back to the bad reputation that the NewGens have been labeled with. Do they deserve it? Are we becoming a nation of narcissists that think they should have it all without really working for it? "In a 2007 survey of 2,500 hiring managers, 87% agreed that younger workers feel more entitled in terms of compensation, benefits, and career advancement than older generations" (Twenge and Campbell, 2009, p. 235).

No one really has a good answer to the question of where all of this narcissistic behavior will lead. "If the narcissism epidemic continues, there will be even more entitlement, materialist, vanity, antisocial behaviors, and relationship problems" (Twenge and Campbell, 2009, p. 277). If people are just expecting things to get done without them having to put forth effort because they are entitled to the results, who will do all of the work?

Some say that we need to change our values and social practices. As parents, we can teach our children that they're not the center of the universe, but how do we teach them that they are special to us without feeling they are overly special compared with the rest of mankind? Every generation faces the problem of how to be the best parents they can be. Hopefully, when NewGens have their own children some day, they'll be able to look at the issues that have come about from too much praise and attention and make some adjustments in how they parent their own children.

Narcissism is just one of many personality disorders that may afflict people. Being narcissistic falls into a category of disorders that may be considered dramatic or erratic. Other personality problems that fall into this category include histrionic or hysterical personality, antisocial personality, and borderline personality.

Those with a hysterical personality disorder may seem overly dramatic. They can be emotional and expressive, and may even come across as childish in behavior. A hypochondriac is a good example of this disorder. For those of you who don't know what a hypochondriac is, it's someone who thinks that everything is making them ill. You know, the person who gets a sore throat and suddenly thinks they have throat cancer ... that's the hypochondriac. They jump to irrational conclusions about illnesses that they talk themselves into thinking they have.

The antisocial personality is your basic sociopath. This person can be quite frightening, because they don't feel guilt or remorse. For those of you who've seen the TV show

Dexter, he's a prime example. Not all sociopaths are killers, but they do tend to rationalize their behaviors and blame others. The good news is, if you work with someone like this, you may not have to do it for very long, because they tend to be antisocial and move from job to job.

The borderline personality group mostly includes women. They tend to have a feeling of abandonment. This is the gal who constantly has problems and issues, goes to the doctor for help, but doesn't think they know what they're doing and ends up quitting therapy. They'd rather complain than actually receive help.

There's another set of personality disorders that may be considered more eccentric or odd in nature. These include paranoid, schizoid, schizotypal personalities. You've probably heard the old joke ... just because you're paranoid doesn't mean they're not out to get you. Well, being paranoid means you think people are out to get you. Because of this, these people don't really let other people get too close to them.

The schizoid is the overly withdrawn, introverted personality. This guy is over in the corner by himself fantasizing, and not letting anyone else into his life. The shizotypal personality is also emotionally detached, but they get into magical thinking. This is the guy who thinks his thoughts can bring an airplane down from the sky.

Another group of personality disorders that we'll discuss here include the inhibited or overly anxious personalities. This would include people who are into avoidance, being dependent, and OCD (obsessive-compulsive disorder) personalities. Those with avoidance issues tend to have social phobias and anxieties. Those with dependent personalities lack self-confidence, and have a hard time making decisions. The OCD personality may seem very orderly, however they have a tough time with change, and need to do things in a specific way. These people sometimes have rituals whereby they have to repeat actions a certain number of times, or avoid things. These people sometimes have rituals whereby they have to repeat actions a certain number of times or avoid things ... oops. You get the picture. The guy who created the saying, "Step on a crack, break your mother's back" probably had OCD!

It would be nice to think that no one at work has any of these extreme personality disorders, however that would probably be considered magical thinking. Unfortunately, there are a lot of people with a lot of issues out there, and so it's important to understand these disorders so that you can recognize them whenever you come into contact with people who have them. The mistake many people make is assuming that everyone is normal, and therefore when they run into someone who isn't, they may blame themselves or drive themselves crazy trying to figure out what they did wrong to get such an irrational or unusual response from that person.

Remember the old saying, "You can please some of the people some of the time but you can't please all of the people all of the time"? If you're trying to have a rational and reasonable relationship with someone who isn't rational or reasonable, you're wasting your time. If you continue to try to change people, or to get them to act in a reasonable fashion, remember another old saying, "The definition of insanity is doing the same thing over and over and expecting a different result." If you're trying to help someone who keeps doing the same thing over and over without getting better, they may have mental health issues.

People with mental disorders often try to manipulate others around them to do the things they want them to do. If you feel you're being manipulated, check out 10 things that Beverly Engel, author of *The Nice Girl Syndrome* (2008), says you can do to protect yourself.

1. Stop Putting Others' Feelings and Needs ahead of Your Own.
2. Stop Believing That Being Nice Will Protect You.
3. Stop Worrying about What Other People Think of You.
4. Stop Trying to Be Perfect.
5. Stop Being Gullible and Naive.
6. Start Standing Up for Your Rights.
7. Start Expressing Your Anger.
8. Learn How to Handle Conflict.
9. Start Facing the Truth about People.
10. Start Supporting and Protecting Yourself.

It can be difficult to tell who has personality disorders. If you find you're constantly helping out people who don't get better, or are always the person taking one for the team, you might want to reassess the situation you're in to see if the people you're interacting with are truly mentally OK. You know how they say that in every group of friends, there's always a crazy one. As the saying goes, look around at your friends, and if you don't know who that crazy one is, it just may be you.

CONCLUSION

"Always be yourself, express yourself, have faith in yourself; do not go out and look for a successful personality and duplicate it."

— Bruce Lee

The one thing that should be extremely evident from reading this book is that there are a lot of ways to measure our personalities. We've covered a lot of them here, but there are many more assessments available out there. In fact, there seems to be a new personality test every time you turn around. Why is this? Perhaps it's because we're eager to learn more about ourselves, and about others. Understanding personalities is also a big area of interest for organizations. As companies are changing how they do business, they're leaning more and more towards team activities. With that change comes the stress of dealing with diversity within these groups. Although we've seen that diversity leads to a more complete group in terms of abilities, it can also lead to serious communication breakdowns.

Even if you're not working in a team atmosphere, you may have to work with other people who have different personalities to you. You may be relying on each other in one way or another to enable each of you to do your jobs. By understanding why people act the way they do, you can adjust not only how you react, but your expectations of your coworkers. This can lead to a much lower level of stress at work.

Of course, understanding these differences can also work for you in your personal life. The more you understand yourself and others, the easier communicating and interrelating will be for you. Personality assessments are utilized all of the time for personal relationships, marriages, parent/child relationships, etc. There are a variety of people we interact with every single day. By understanding how to adjust our expectations of others, we have a better chance of accepting others and getting along with one another.

One question you may be asking is, If there are so many tests and definitions of personality, how do I know which one is the best or the right one? That is indeed the big question, and the answer is, there really isn't one right test or definition out there. The best you can do is to understand that there are many different ideas about how we think and act and, as you might have noticed, many of these theories overlap, and have similar components to them.

To save you spending all of your money taking each and every one of these tests, we've covered some of the top assessments here so that you can see the basic premise behind each one. You may be interested in going ahead and taking some of them to better understand yourself, or you may feel you can figure out where you fit by reading the definitions. Even more importantly, you may be able to see where someone else fits, to help explain why they act the way they do. Your personality won't always match the personality of others around you, but by realizing that we all have different personalities and preferences, you can better adjust your inter-relationship style as you come to recognize certain personality traits in your coworkers, family and friends.

By doing this, you can be more productive and less frustrated in the work environment, and enjoy better personal relationships. By understanding personalities, you can not only work on how you present yourself to others, but also be more patient by understanding why other people are so annoying. Hopefully, now that you've learned about analyzing personalities, you'll be better able to read your coworkers, family members, and friends. It's important to try to focus on your similarities and take advantage of combining your differences for a more diverse and richer experience. You can also utilize this information to work on areas that need improvement. By improving yourself, you may open yourself up to being more promotable, more likable, and better marrying material. By having this knowledge, you can win at the personality game.

REFERENCES

Baron, R. (1998) What Type Am I: Discover Who You Really Are. New York, The Penguin Group.

Birkman.com (2009) Retrieved December 17, 2009 from http://www.birkman.com/news/babyboomers.pdf.

Blass, T. (2004) The Man Who Shocked the World: The Life and Legacy of Stanley Milgram. New York. Basic Books.

Blifalo.com (2009) Retrieved December 17, 2009 from http://www.blifaloo.com/humor/freud.php.

Bnet.com (2009) Retrieved December 17, 2009 from Bnet.com

Boston College (2006) Retrieved December 17, 2009 from http://www.bc.edu/research/agingandwork/.

BusinessBalls.com (2009) Retrieved December 30, 2009 from http://www.businessballs.com/personalitystylesmodels.htm.

CBS News (2007) Retrieved December 17, 2009 from http://www.cbsnews.com/stories/2007/11/08/60minutes/main3475200.shtml.

CPP.com (2009) The Strong Assessment. Strong Interest Inventory Assessment Helps Your Clients Identify, Understand, and Expand Their Career Options, Retrieved December 29, 2009 from www.cpp.com.

Demarais, A. and White, V. (2004) First Impressions: What You Don't Know About How Others See You. New York, Bantam Dell.

DiscoverYourPersonality.com (2009) Retrieved December 17, 2009 from http://www.discoveryourpersonality.com/Strong.html.

Donnay, D. et al. (2004) Technical Brief for the Newly Revised STRONG Interest Inventory Assessment, www.cpp.com.

Engel, B. (2008) The Nice Girl Syndrome: Stop Being Manipulated and Abused -- and Start Standing Up for Yourself. New York, Wiley Publishing.

Erickson, T. (2009) Retrieved December 17, 2009 from http://blogs.harvardbusiness.org/erickson/2009/07/why_generation_x_has_the_leade.html.

Facesearch.org. (2009) Retrieved December 17, 2009 from http://www.faceresearch.org/.

Farr, M. and Shatkin, L. (2009) Fifty Best Jobs for Your Personality. Indiana, Jist Publishing.

Furnham, A. (2008) Personality and Intelligence at Work: Exploring and Explaining Individual Differences at Work. New York, Routledge.

Guadagno, R.E. et al. (2007) Who blogs? Personality predictors of blogging, Computers in Human Behavior.

Halcyon.com (2009) Retrieved December 17, 2009 from http://www.halcyon.com/jmashmun/npd/dsm-iv.html.

Hammill, G. (2005) Retrieved December 17, 2009 from http://www.fdu.edu/newspubs/magazine/05ws/generations.htm.

Harmon, L. Hansen, J. Borgen, F. and Hammer, A. (1994) Strong Interest Inventory: Applications and Technical Guide. California, Stanford University Press.

Hartman, T. (2009) Retrieved December 17, 2009 from http://www.colorcode.com/personality_test/.

Helium.com (2009) Retrieved January 06, 2010 from http://www.helium.com/items/1243327-personality-and-zodiac-your-zodiac-and-personality-the-personality-of-each-zodiac-sign.

Hicks, R. and Hicks, K. (1999) Boomers, Xers and Other Strangers: Understanding the Generational Differences That Divide Us. Illinois, Tyndale House Publishers.

Hodo.com (2010) Retrieved July 6, 2010 from http://www.hodu.com/EQ.shtml.

Hogan, R. (2007) Personality and the Fate of Organizations. New Jersey, Lawrence Erlbaum Associates.

Hogan, T. (2007) Psychological Testing: A Practical Introduction. New Jersey, John Wiley and Sons.

HolyMoly.com (2009) Retrieved December 17, 2009 from http://www.holymoly.com/page/NewsDetail/0,,12643~1604083,00.html.

Honore, S. and Schofield, C. (2009) Retrieved December 17, 2009 from http://www.ashridge.org.uk/Website/IC.nsf/wFARATT/Generation%20Y%3A%20Inside%20Out.%20A%20multi-generational%20view%20of%20Generation%20Y%20-%20learning%20and%20working/$File/GenerationYInsideOut.pdf.

Hotchkiss, S. (2003) Why is it Always About You? The Seven Deadly Sins of Narcissism. New York, Free Press.

Howard, P. and Howard, J. (2001) The Owner's Manual for Personality at Work. Texas, Bard Press.

Hughes, R., Ginnett, R. and Curphy, G. (2009) Leadership: Enhancing the Lessons of Experience. Boston, McGraw-Hill.

Institute for Motivational Living (2008) Introduction to Behavioral Analysis IML Certification Guide. Pennsylvania, The Institute for Motivational Living.

John, O., Robins, R. and Pervin, L. (2008) Handbook of Personality: Theory and Research. New York, The Guilford Press.

Keirsey.com (2009) Retrieved December 17, 2009 from http://www.keirsey.com/brains.aspx.

Kolbe, K. (1997) Conative Connection: Acting on Instinct. Massachusetts, Kathy Kolbe.

Kroeger, O. (2002) Type Talk at Work: How the 16 Personality Types Determine Your Success on the Job. New York, Dell Publishing.

Leman, K. (2009) The Birth Order Book: Why You Are the Way You Are. Michigan, Baker Publishing Group.

Leman, K. (2009) Birth Order Facts and Your Personality: 8 Facts That Might Surprise You. Retrieved January 5, 2010 from http://www.ivillage.co.uk/relationships/famfri/family/articles/0,,163_559974,00.html.

Lifescript.com (2009) Retrieved December 17, 2009 from www.Lifescript.com.

MBS (2009) Retrieved December 17, 2009 from www.strengths.com.

MentalHealth.net (2009) Retrieved December 17, 2009 from http://www.mentalhelp.net/poc/view_doc.php/type/doc/id/419.

Most, R. and Zeidner, M. (1995) Psychologist Testing: An Inside View.

MyersBriggs.org (2009) Retrieved December 17, 2009 from www.MyersBriggs.org.

Nettle, D. (2007) Personality: What Makes You The Way You Are. New York, Oxford University Press.

Newstrategist.com (2009) Retrieved December 17, 2009 from http://www.newstrategist.com/productdetails/Gen5SamplePgs.pdf.

Osborne, W., Brown, S., Niles, S. and Miner, C. (1997) Career Development, Assessment and Counseling: Applications of the Donald E. Super C-DAC Approach. Virginia, American Counseling Association.

Pinsky, D. and Young, S. (2009) The Mirror Effect: How Celebrity Narcissism is Seducing America. New York, Harper.

Pyschinaction.com (2009) Retrieved December 17, 2009 from www.psychinaction.com/uimages//78.doc.

Rath, T. (2007) Strengths Finder 2.0. New York, Gallup Press.

RobertHalfInternational.com (2010) Retrieved December 17, 2009 from http://www.rhi.com/GenY.

Robinson (2006) Retrieved December 17, 2009 from http://www.highbeam.com/doc/1G1-149520307.html.

Salovey, P., Brackett, M. and Mayer, J. (2007). Emotional Intelligence: Key Readings on Mayer and Salovey Model. New York. Dude Publishing.

Scribd.com (2009) Retrieved December 17, 2009 from http://www.scribd.com/doc/2607132/GENERATION-Y-THE-MILLENNIALS.

SignalPatterns.com (2009) Retrieved December 17, 2009 from www.signalpatterns.com.

Slater, L. (2004) Opening Skinner's Box. Great psychological Experiments of the Twentieth Century. New York, W.W. Norton & Co.

Swangroup.co (2009) Retrieved December 17, 2009 from http://www.swanngroup.co.nz/articles/Dark-Side-Personality-Leadership.pdf.

Sweeney, R. (2006) Retrieved December 17, 2009 from http://library1.njit.edu/staff-folders/sweeney/Millennials/Article-Millennial-Behaviors.doc.

TheFreedictionary.com (2009)

Tieger, P. and Barron, B. (2007) Do What You Are: Discover the Perfect Career for You Through the Secrets of Personality Type. New York. Little, Brown and Company.

Twenge, J. (2006) Generation Me: Why Today's Young Americans Are More Confident, Assertive, Entitle—and More Miserable Than Ever Before. New York, The Free Press.

Twenge, J. and Campbell, W. (2009) Living in the age of Entitlement: The Narcissism Epidemic. New York, Free Press.

Vancouver Sun (2009) Retrieved December 17, 2009 from http://www.canada.com/vancouversun/news/business/story.html?id=69221809-a423-4168-b1ae-01564eeb8aab&k=45631&utm_

Made in the USA
Las Vegas, NV
31 August 2021